Dynamics of U.S. Public Policies

Understanding American Politics Today

Political Affairs & Government Relations

ISBN: 979-8-646891786

References: Thomas Patterson, PhD

U.S. Public Policies
Social, Economic and Foreign Policy

TABLE OF CONTENTS

Foreword

References

Comparative Politics of American Public Policies

Foreword

Many Americans are confused about embracing both a knee-jerk hostility to government while embracing much of what government actually does. This has to do with the anti-government rhetoric that has gained ascendance in recent decades. This book slashes through the ideological haze to show citizens, the achievements of, and yes, the concerns surrounding politics of the American government.

This book is to merely educate and help citizens to fully understand what their government does, in order to make up their own minds on policy-related issues. In my opinion, understanding American politics today, requires us to understand the principles from the founding documents, the Declaration of Independence, and the Constitution.

Of course, they do not explain everything about today's politics. But no accounting of today's politics would be complete without bringing them into the story. This is why, taking a look at some dynamics of American politics such as the Social, Economic and Foreign Policies is vital, especially when heading in that direction.

Thomas Patterson, PhD

Harvard University's Kennedy School of Government

Social Policy

When we think of political issues, we tend to think of guns and butter, which is a shorthand way of talking about national security and economic policy issues. But they are not the only issues on our minds. Social issues concern us as well.

Social issues refer to disputes over values. One social issue, slavery, nearly tore the country apart in the 19th century. Another social issue, alcohol, was the subject of a 20th century constitutional amendment that backfired. Rather than ushering in an era of sobriety, it opened the door to bootleggers, speakeasies, and gangsters. Social issues are divisive. They pit people against people.

Think about the conflicts today over such social issues as immigration, charter schools, gun rights, legalization of marijuana, television violence and nudity, climate change, and discrimination of all kinds. Such disputes involve the question of what type of society the United States should aspire to be.

Americans are divided on that question. A recent Pew Research Center poll asked Americans, whether they consider themselves to be liberal or conservative on social issues. As it turned out, Americans are split right down the middle. The number who said they are conservative on social issues was matched by the number who said they are liberal. We will also discuss several social issues, none more fully than discrimination, which was the focus of our approach on civil rights, and that was talked about in other relevant books as well.

In this segment, we will be discussing social issues through the lens of religion. Over the course of American history, no aspect of society has played more directly into social issues than has religion. Social issues arise out of differences in values, and religions are rooted in values. Not surprisingly, the intersection of religion and politics has been a major source of conflict within the American system.

In the United States, religion plays a larger political role than it does in nearly every other Western democracy. One does not have to search far for the reason. Americans are a religious people.

Focusing on religion as a source of political conflict is important because it deals with social issues. That focus is typical when studying politics, which political scientist Harold Lasswell described as conflict over who gets what, when, and how. Conflict is not the only story to tell about religion in the United States. The violent religious episodes that in recent decades have rocked many countries from Northern Ireland, to Nigeria, to Iraq, to Pakistan, are rarer in the United States. It is not that they do not happen. In the aftermath of the terrorist attacks on US soil on September 11, 2001, the FBI recorded a sharp spike in Muslim-related hate crimes, including beatings, arson, and several killings. But the frequency and scale of such incidents is not anything like that found in many parts of the world. Now why, apart from America's law enforcement system, is that the case?

In their book called "*American Grace, How Religion Divides and Unites Us*", scholars Robert Putnam and David Campbell provided us one of the answers. They conducted a multi-year study, interviewing and re-interviewing several thousand Americans to assess the part that religion plays in their lives. Putnam and Campbell found that most Americans have two or more close friends and at least one extended family member of a different faith.

Such relationships were found to promote religious tolerance. Even new friendships with people of a different religion were found to lead to greater acceptance of that religious faith. Such interactions are common in the US because of its religious diversity. America is divided among so many religious denominations that contact with individuals of other faiths is unavoidable for most people. The situation is different in countries where religious faiths are separated by geographical location or social arrangements. In those cases, there is less mixing of religions. The effect can be an in-group, out-group mentality that breeds religious hostility. That is true even of the 10% or so of Americans who live in tight-knit religious communities. Putnam and Campbell found them to have relatively high levels of religious intolerance.

Putnam and Campbell's findings are supported by a recent Pew Research Center survey. Poll respondents were found to have a more positive opinion of another religion if they knew someone who practiced it. It is a reason that the religions Islam, Buddhism, and Hinduism of many of America's newer immigrants are viewed less positively than long-established U.S. religions.

Fewer Americans know someone who practices these religions. The Muslim religion ranked lowest in the Pew survey, reflecting its association, in some Americans' minds, with terrorism. But even that reaction is diluted by social interaction. The Pew survey found that Americans who personally knew a Muslim had a significantly higher opinion of Islam than those who did not. There is an old saying in America, familiarity breeds contempt. That might be true in some areas of life. But it is not true when it comes to religion. It is also not true when it comes to politics. Studies show that Americans who frequently interact with people of the other party, and who are frequently exposed to both sides of political debate, hold more moderate political opinions than those who are politically isolated. A recent New York University study found that to be true also of virtual interaction. Facebook and Twitter users in politically diverse networks tend to hold more moderate political views than those who are not. Alexis de Tocqueville, the French observer who wrote about American society in the 1830s, was one of the first to note the importance of social interaction. For Tocqueville, democracy was a social condition as well as a political condition and a legal condition. Tocqueville wrote, "If men are to remain civilized, the art of associating together must grow.

The Pew Research Center cross-national survey found that American respondents were far more likely than Italian, German, Spanish, or French respondents to say that religion is particularly important in their lives. Religion in America is at once uniform and diverse.

It is uniform in the sense that the country is overwhelmingly Christian. It has the most Christians of any country. The Jewish community also has deep roots in American society but accounts for only 2% of the population. Other non-Christians, including Muslims, Hindus and Buddhists, are increasing in number, but together they account for less than 3% of the American population.

At the same time, America's Christians are religiously diverse. Catholics are the largest single denomination numbering more than 60 million, but even so, they make up only about 25% of the population. Protestants outnumber them by roughly two to one but are split among more than 200 denominations. The largest is the Southern Baptist Convention with roughly 16 million members, more than 90% of whom are white. Second, with 8 and 1/2 million members, is the National Baptist Convention and nearly all black denomination that broke with the Southern Baptist during the era of racial segregation.

Both denominations are evangelical, meaning that they practice evangelism, the spreading of the Gospel to others and regard the Bible as the literal word of God. Other Protestant faiths place less emphasis on evangelism and the Bible as a literal text. The largest of the so-called mainline Protestant religions is the United Methodist Church with 8 million members. At one time, mainline Protestants were in the majority. Today, they are outnumbered by evangelicals. Religions differ in doctrine, a term that refers to how they instruct their followers on such things as the nature of the universe, the path to salvation, and the proper way to conduct their lives. The Catholic and Jewish religions, for example, stress the importance of good works, particularly in helping the poor, the sick and the weak.

While Protestants do so, by an emphasis on self-reliance, what Max Weber called the Protestant ethic.

Among Protestants, there is a split, with mainline denominations placing more emphasis on good works, the so-called social Gospel, while evangelical denominations place more emphasis on personal faith, the individual Gospel. These differences in doctrine are not sharply defined even within each tradition there is considerable variation.

Nevertheless, they can affect how their followers respond to politics. For example, in a survey that asked Americans whether government should see to it that every person has a job and a good standard of living, Jewish and Catholic respondents, consistent with their religious doctrines, were most likely to agree, followed by mainline Protestants, with evangelical Protestants the least likely to hold that opinion.

Let us look at the influence of religion on American politics, starting with religion's impact in the period before the Great Depression. Religious conflict in this period was largely sectarian, Protestants against Catholics. Including the religion's emergence in the 1970s as a powerful political force in response to issues such as abortion and same sex marriage.

The First Amendment says that "Congress shall make no law respecting an establishment of religion or prohibiting the free exercise thereof." The First Amendment did not, however keep, religion from working its way into American politics. Indeed, historians and political scientists have concluded that next to race, religion was the leading issue of 19th century politics in America.

In the nation's earlier decades, religion was a progressive force. Churches were behind the drive to create public schools and charity houses. They also sparked the abolitionist movement, arguing that slavery was a sin of the highest order and a betrayal of the nation's promise.

Said Angelina Grimke, a leading abolitionist, "God punished Egypt and Judea because of slavery and have we any reason to believe that he will spare America?" The debate over slavery was so intense within some denominations that it led them to split into pro and anti-slavery branches. These efforts were to continue.

Churches were also to provide leadership on women's suffrage. But religion in the 19th century also had its dark side. In the 1840s, religion in America took a sharp turn of a reactionary nature. Economic hardship in Ireland had suddenly brought large numbers of Irish Catholics to America. At the time of the American Revolution, the United States was 99% Protestant. Even as late as 1840, it was more than 95% Protestant. Most of them were not happy with the prospect of sharing their country with Irish Catholics.

Today, we think of race largely in terms of blacks and whites. In the 19th century, race was a bigger category.

The Irish were considered by established Americans to belong to a different race, an inferior one in the minds of many. Said George Templeton Strong, a prominent lawyer and writer, "The Irish are almost as remote from us as are the Chinese." The Catholic influx gave rise to the Know-Nothing Party, or as it was officially called, the American Party. The party's platform called for public schools to hold daily Bible readings and to ban Catholic teachers. In the 1856 election, the American Party's presidential nominee, former president Millard Fillmore, attracted nearly 25% of the vote, the second highest third-party total in the nation's history.

Anti-Catholic sentiment was particularly strong in small towns and rural areas, which in the North after the Civil War were Republican strongholds. Urban areas were more tolerant. And Catholics became the backbone of the Democratic Party organizations in New York, Boston, and other cities. The 19th century religious divide can be seen in this chart. Northern Catholics were heavily Democratic. The margin was four to one. While northern Protestants of every denomination were Republican, some by a very wide margin. White Protestants in the South, where race trumped religion, were the exception. They were Democrats as a result of the Republican Party's role in freeing the slaves.

Now in the late 19th and early 20th centuries, the United States experienced its largest wave of immigration in history. Most of it from Southern and Eastern Europe. The Catholic population tripled as a result, while the Jewish population increased eightfold. To old line Americans, this influx threatens the nation's well-being. A congressional report labeled Eastern European Jews as mentally diffusion and socially undesirable, concluding that 85% to 90% of them lack any conception of patriotic or national spirit. The Protestant backlash led to the rebirth of the Ku Klux Klan. Formed in the South after the Civil War to repress the newly freed slaves, The Klan was so violent that it lost support even in the South and by 1900 had virtually disappeared.

It was resurrected in 1915 as an organization that was anti-Catholic, anti-Jewish, and anti-Mormon, as well as anti-black. The new Klan succeeded beyond its founders' wildest dreams. At peak, one in every six Protestant white males in the United States was a Klan member. Indiana, a non-Southern state had the largest membership. Klan organizers would go into a city, sign up new members, and cap off the recruitment with a huge rally marked by the burning of a cross and the ceremonial gift of a Bible to a prominent local Protestant.

The Klan's political power was on full display at the 1924 Democratic National Convention when it blocked the presidential nomination of Alfred Smith, the governor of New York and a Catholic. The Klan's choice was one of its own, William McAdoo, who had been President Woodrow Wilson's Treasury Secretary and had married his daughter. McAdoo was backed by Democratic delegates from Southern and rural states, while Smith had the support of delegates from Northern, urban states.

Now, in those days, it took a 2/3 vote of the delegates to win the nomination. The balloting went on for days, with neither Smith nor McAdoo reaching the threshold. Finally, they both withdrew, resulting in the nomination of a political unknown on John W. Davis on the 103rd ballot.

It was the longest party convention in US history. To celebrate Smith's defeat, the Klan organized a rally that drew thousands of its members, dressed in the Klan's traditional hooded cape. Four years later, Smith won the Democratic presidential nomination but lost the election in a landslide amid charges he was an agent of the pope. For the first time since the Civil War, Republicans carried the heavily Protestant states of Texas, Virginia, and North Carolina and nearly swept the whole of the South. Religious bigotry was not confined to politics.

Many colleges refused to schedule football games with Notre Dame, a Catholic institution. Twice Notre Dame's application to join the Big 10 football conference was voted down by anti-Catholic coaches and university administrators. As important as religion was in the 1928 election, its power diminished soon thereafter. The Great Depression had hit, and Americans were far more concerned with their pocket than with their neighbor's religion. The nation's entry into World War II, where Americans of all faiths fought side by side, further eroded religious resentments. As historian *Thomas Bruscino* noted, the war produced a sea change in religious relations. "The war," he wrote, "remade the nation."

The change in Americans' attitudes was reflected in the increased rate of interfaith marriage. The rate of Protestant-Catholic marriages doubled in the 1950s from its earlier level. Although religion was seldom an issue in 1950s politics, America's political parties retained a religious flavor. Most Catholics and Jews supported the Democratic Party. And most northern Protestants backed the GOP. Although Democrats, as a result of Franklin Roosevelt's New Deal, had made inroads with younger and blue-collar Protestants. Then in 1960, religion came back into play when Democrats picked John F. Kennedy, a Catholic, as their presidential nominee.

Kennedy sought to assure Protestant voters about his religion. Said Kennedy, "I am not the Catholic candidate for president. I am the Democratic Party's candidate for president, who also happens to be a Catholic. I do not speak for my church on public matters and the church does not speak for me." A study by scholars at MIT estimated that Kennedy's religion cost him 1.5 million votes nationwide and tipped the states of California, Kentucky, Oklahoma, and Tennessee into the Republican column.

Despite that, Kennedy's religion may actually have won him the election. Heavy Catholic turnout enabled him to pick up the states of New York, Connecticut, Pennsylvania, and Illinois. They had 22 more electoral votes than the four states he lost because of his religion. Kennedy's presidency and his assassination three years later virtually closed the chapter on the conflict between America's Protestants and Catholics. When John Kerry ran for the presidency in 2004, the first Catholic presidential nominee since Kennedy, his religion was barely mentioned. Although the 1960s ended one form of religious conflict, it planted the seeds of another. In 1962, the Supreme Court ruled that prayer in the public schools violated the First Amendment's establishment clause. A year later, the Court barred Bible readings in the public schools.

Then in 1965, the Supreme Court, citing a right to privacy, held that states could not prohibit the use of birth control pills, which had been approved for contraceptive use by the Food and Drug Administration. That ruling was followed by another right to privacy ruling in 1973.

In Roe v. Wade the Supreme Court held that abortion was legal during the first trimester of pregnancy. Religious conservatives were dismayed by these rulings and also by the women's rights movement that had formed out of the Civil Rights movement and by the counterculture movement with its emphasis on drugs and sexual liberation that had developed out of the anti-Vietnam War movement. In the view of religious conservatives, the traditional male-headed family and the nation's religious values were under attack. A fault line emerged, secularists and the more liberal religious denominations on one side of the culture debate and the more conservative religious denominations on the other side. In response to what he described as the nation's moral decay, the Reverend Jerry Falwell, a minister of the Southern Baptist Convention, founded the Moral Majority. Headquartered in Virginia with chapters in every Southern state and built around a network of evangelical ministers, the Moral Majority, at peak, had more than 4 million members and nearly two million donors.

The Moral Majority's program called for restoring Christian prayer in the public schools, outlawing abortion, preserving the traditional family, boycotting media outlets that carried sexual content, and opposing the Equal Rights Amendment, which would have formerly granted women the same constitutional status as men.

In 1980 and 1984, the Moral Majority endorsed Republican Ronald Reagan's presidential candidacy and spent millions on televised advertising and voter registration drives aimed at securing his election. The Christian right's role in Republican politics was further strengthened when the Reverend Pat Robertson, a Baptist minister who founded the Christian Broadcasting Network, ran for the 1988 Republican presidential nomination. He lost but ran strongly in the early contests and brought tens of thousands of evangelical Christians into the activist ranks of the Republican Party.

Soon thereafter, Robertson created the Christian Coalition with chapters in every state. By the mid-1990s, its members held leadership positions in a third of the state Republican Party organizations. Religious ferment after Roe v. Wade resulted in a denominational realignment. In the 1976 presidential election, evangelical Christians had divided their vote evenly between the Republican and Democratic presidential nominees.

In 1980, Reagan's first election, more than 60% of evangelicals voted Republican.

In 1984 and then again in 1988, roughly 80% of them did so. Less dramatic but significant changes had also taken place among other religious groups. Catholics had become a less reliable source of Democratic votes. Those who went to church regularly were now casting most of their votes for Republican candidates.

As political scientist John Green noted, "There isn't a Catholic vote anymore. There are several Catholic votes." Meanwhile, secularists and liberal mainline Protestants were increasingly voting Democratic. The party's national platform reflected the change.

In 1976, the Republican platform had a plank calling for a ban on abortion. Every Republican platform since has included such a plan. The 1976 Democratic platform had a plank endorsing a woman's right to choose.

Every Democratic platform since has had such a plank. Now in the 1990s, Democratic Party leaders began to vigorously contest the growing power of the religious right, centering their push on women's rights and taking up the issue of gay rights.

During the 1992 presidential campaign, Democratic nominee Bill Clinton proposed to end the ban on gays and lesbians in the armed services. At their national party convention, Republican speakers played up Clinton's position, declaring it an assault on family values. As a political issue, same-sex relations had advantages for both parties. Gays and lesbians were increasingly outspoken in their demand for equal treatment. Their sexual identity was central enough that many were willing to vote on it.

According to exit polls, Clinton received roughly 80% of the 1992 two-party vote of gays and lesbians. The appeal to women's rights was also a source of Democratic votes. Clinton won 56% of the two-party vote among women. A gender gap, the difference in the vote preferences of men and women, had opened in the 1980s, and the 1990s solidified it. Ever since, Democratic candidates at the congressional as well as at the presidential level have run more strongly among women than men. But gender also gave conservatives a potent issue. Referring to same-sex relations, the Reverend Lou Sheldon, head of the Traditional Values Coalition, said, "We now have another front burner issue in addition to abortion." Republican lawmakers also recognized the potential of the same-sex issue. In nearly every state, they introduced bills defining marriage as the union between a man and a woman.

By 2001, a majority of states had adopted a statute or constitutional amendment upholding traditional marriage.

In the 2004 elections, Republicans placed a marriage referendum on the ballot in 13 states, expecting it to draw religious conservatives to the polls. It worked. And in every case, the referendum passed easily.

The same strategy was pursued two years later in the nine states. If there was any question about the degree to which religion had been absorbed into American politics, it was dispelled by the composition of the vote in the 2000 and 2004 presidential elections.

Among voters who went to church regularly, Republican candidate George W. Bush received more than 60% of the vote in 2000. Among infrequent and non-attendees, he got less than 40% of the vote. That same 60/40 pattern occurred again in the 2004 election. The increasingly close relationship between religion and party can also be seen in the trend in party identification. In the early '70s, there was basically no correlation between the frequency of church attendance and America's party loyalties. Since then, the correlation has increased, with regular churchgoers loyal to the Republican Party. Now, where are things headed?

What role is religion likely to play in the nation's politics in the years ahead? There are some signs that religious-based conflict could be weakening. Some prominent evangelical leaders believe it was a mistake to tie religion so closely to politics, particularly in light of the fact that it did not produce many policy victories.

They would refocus the Christian right on its evangelical mission, contending that it is close identification with the Republican Party has made it harder to preach the Gospel to Democratic leaning Americans, Hispanics particularly. Some observers also point to the same-sex marriage issue as a possible sign of religion's weakening influence. In the entire history of polling, there have been few issues where public opinion has changed so dramatically in such a short period as has been true of Americans' opinions on gay marriage. In the early 1990s, fewer than 20% of Americans back same-sex marriage. Even a decade later, support was exceptionally low. Today, a majority of Americans approve of same-sex marriage. Remarkably, unlike the abortion issue where Republicans and Democrats have shifted in opposite directions, support for same-sex marriage has increased among Republicans and Democrats alike.

There is a wide gap in their opinions on the issue, but the trend for both is upward. That is also true for religious groups, as you can see in this figure. Although white evangelicals are predictably the most opposed to gay marriage, they, like the other religious groups, have become more supportive of it.

In 2015, the Supreme Court ruled that same-sex couples have a constitutional right to marry, thereby extending the practice to all 50 states. Although the Court's decision could conceivably intensify opposition to same-sex marriage, the public's response to previous civil rights rulings, suggests that the decision is more likely to reduce opposition to such marriages.

On the other hand, the religious issue surfaced in force during the 2016 presidential election after Donald Trump said Muslims should be barred from entering the United States. Although Trump later qualified his position, one of his first actions as president was to try to block the entry of Muslims from several Middle East countries, while allowing the entry of non-Muslim immigrants, including Christians, from the same countries.

A Reuters poll found that roughly half the American public agreed with Trump and have disagreed, with the opinion split sharply along party lines.

Republicans were three times as likely as Democrats to agree when asked whether banning people from Muslim countries is necessary to prevent terrorism. Thus, it is an open question whether religion is weakening as a political force. What is clear is that it is not going to disappear anytime soon. The abortion issue by itself virtually guarantees it. In the four decades since Roe v. Wade, abortion issues have not changed much in the aggregate. The proportions of pro-life and pro-choice Americans today are roughly the same as they were in the 1970s. What has different today is how these opinions align with Americans partisanship. As you can see in this figure, Republicans have become increasingly anti-abortion, while Democrats have moved in the opposite direction. Republicans and Democrats are now far apart, polarized, on the abortion issue. Religion is a component of the party realignment we discussed earlier. Today's party coalitions are markedly different than they were at a time when Catholics were reliably Democratic and Protestants reliably Republican. Differences in religious belief about personal morality, the nature of the family, the need for religious observance, and the like count for more than religious labels when it comes to Americans' party loyalties.

As Putnam and Campbell argue, how religious a person is, has become more important as a political dividing line than which denomination he or she belongs to. That observation was born out in the 2012 election. The Republican candidate Mitt Romney was the first Mormon to win presidential nomination. Although polls indicate that white evangelicals, more than any other religious group, question the validity of the Mormon religion, it did not stop them from backing Romney. Exit polls found that he received 79% of the white evangelical vote, an amount equal to that of George W. Bush in 2004 and six percentage points higher than John McCain in 2008.

To white evangelicals, Romney's positions on abortion, same-sex marriage, and other social issues easily trumped his denomination. Party loyalties and religious beliefs are now interlocked. It is hard to imagine what, if anything, will break that bond in the foreseeable future. As this figure shows, what is true of religion is true of social issues generally. Most Republicans describe themselves as social conservatives, while most Democrats call themselves social liberals. The tendency is pronounced enough to suggest that social issues in one form or another are likely to be a source of partisan conflict for years to come. OK, let us summarize what I talked about in this segment about religion and politics.

As we began by noting that despite the constitutional separation of church and state, religion was a powerful force in early American politics, finding expression in sectarian conflict, the dominant Protestant population against the growing number of Catholics. This conflict worked its way into the party system, with Catholics identifying with the Democratic Party and northern Protestants with the Republican Party. The heavily Protestant South, where race rather than religion was the top issue, was the exception.

The Great Depression and World War II served to reduce Protestant-Catholic antagonisms, which were further diminished after John F. Kennedy's election in 1960. Since then, religion's political influence has come in response to issues such as school prayer, abortion, and family norms. These issues serve to mobilize religious conservatives, who are aligned with, and were embraced by the Republican Party. Meanwhile, seculars and religious progressives increasingly sided with the Democratic Party. Religious observance and party identification are now tightly linked.

Fiscal Monetary Policy

The Federal Reserve Bank was established in 1913, nearly a half century before monetary theory was developed. The Fed's early history has some interesting twists.

The Fed's origins traced to the bank panic of 1907, which threatened to collapse the banking system and take the economy down with it. Today, when we hear the word "bankrupt," we think of an individual or firm going bankrupt. But the word originated in the times when it was banks that went bankrupt. "Bankrupt" literally means "broken bank." To make money, banks take in deposits and then loan them out.

If a bank held on to all of the money deposited with it, it could not make a profit. But the fact that banks loan out most of their assets means that at any given time they have less money on hand than they owe their depositors. If people panic and think their money is no longer safe in their bank, they will rush to take it out. Soon, the bank will have given out all the cash it had on hand. Other depositors will be out of luck and the bank will have gone bankrupt.

That is what was happening in 1907, and as one bank after another closed, the panic was spreading. At this point, JP Morgan, a top financier of his time, called together a group of his rich friends and convinced them to put money into a pool from which banks could borrow if they started running short on cash.

Morgan's plan worked. The panic subsided. But JP Morgan's solution lingered in policymakers' minds. Why not create a permanent government bank from which bankers could borrow? JP Morgan became the strongest advocate for creating the Federal Reserve. Other leading bankers of the era opposed the idea, including John Jacob Astor, Benjamin Guggenheim, and Isa Straus. Astor, the world's wealthiest man, was the leading critic. Their feud with Morgan became grist for conspiracy theorists after the Titanic sank on its maiden voyage in 1912. Astor, Guggenheim and Straus all went down with the ship. Morgan had been booked on the Titanic but canceled his trip at the last minute. Interestingly, Morgan was an owner of the ship and had insured it against loss. Adding to the conspiracy stew was the fact that a decade before the Titanic sank, a novelist had written a book that described almost exactly the conditions that doomed the Titanic - hitting an iceberg and killing most of those on board because there weren't enough lifeboats.

When that author was then poisoned to death, the claim that Morgan had a hand in the sinking of the Titanic grew. Now, like all conspiracy theories, this one is way short on facts and way long on imagination. But it is fascinating, nonetheless. Even today, when you go online, you find bizarre accounts of how the Federal Reserve was made possible by the sinking of the Titanic.

Ever since the 1930s, the federal government has taken responsibility for managing the nation's economy, keeping unemployment and inflation in check. The Fed is part of that effort. So, too, is Congress, through its taxing and spending policies. But increasingly, the responsibility is shifted over to the Fed. Its economic tools can be more effectively targeted, more quickly applied, than the tools available to Congress. Few events have had a bigger impact on US policy than the 1930s Great Depression. In response to the economic crisis, the federal government provided a safety net for the economically weak and tightened its regulation of business. Among the federal agencies created during the Depression were the Securities and Exchange Commission, which regulates the stock and bond markets, and the Social Security Administration, which administers the Social Security program.

The Great Depression also changed policymakers' thinking about the government's role in the economy. Before then, the government had more or less kept its hands off the economy, letting it go through a natural cycle of ups and downs. Every few decades, the economy would take a nosedive. Prevailing theory held that it would eventually self-correct, launching another period of prosperity. But since the Depression, the government has actively managed the economy, seeking to keep it on a more even keel.

In this section, I would like to look at two major policy approaches to this effort: fiscal policy, which refers to the government's taxing and spending decisions, carried out by Congress and the president. In such discussion, it is important to look at alternative approaches to fiscal policy demand-side policy, which is based largely on government spending levels, and supply-side policy, based on tax levels.

Also, to discuss monetary policy, which involves adjusting the money supply in response to economic conditions. Monetary policy is exercised primarily through the Federal Reserve. Now, when the economy weakens, firms and consumers behave in ways that contribute to the economic downturn.

Faced with declining demand for their goods, firms cut back on production, which accelerates the job loss. Meanwhile, consumers pull back on their spending, which weakens demand for goods, resulting in further job loss.

So, before the Great Depression, government action also added to the downward spiral. Confronted with declining tax revenues as a result of deteriorating incomes and profits, government would cut back its spending, further accelerating the job loss and the slowing of business activity. The British economist John Maynard Keynes argued that government was doing exactly the opposite of what it should do. Instead of cutting back on spending, he argued, government should increase it. By doing so, government would put money into consumers' hands, which, when spent, would stimulate job growth and production. Keynesian fiscal policy centered on the demand side of the supply-demand relationship. Increase the level of aggregate demand, the amount of money consumers is spending, and the effect will be an increase in aggregate supply, and the amount producers are supplying. That notion drove some of President Franklin Roosevelt's 1930s New Deal programs. For example, the Works Progress Administration (WPA) employed millions of jobless Americans on public works projects.

New parks, bridges and other facilities were built in hundreds of American cities and towns. The workers' pay fed into the economy, boosting production, which led to job hires. Now, not everyone backed such programs. Economic conservatives said government had no business meddling in the markets. By the 1950s, that argument was fading.

A consequence of demand-side fiscal policy, a bigger federal government, remained an issue, particularly among Republican lawmakers.

Accordingly, when Republican Ronald Reagan became president in 1981 in the midst of an economic recession, the jobless rate had reached a post-war high of 11%. He chose an alternative approach. Reagan targeted the supply side, convincing Congress to give the large tax break to business and upper income taxpayers. Reagan's logic was that if business and the wealthy had more money, they would invest in production, the supply side of the economic equation. To increase production, business would have to hire more workers. Their pay would then feed into the economy, stimulating further production, and hiring.

Reagan's supply-side approach came to be called trickle-down economics, the idea that greater wealth at the top of society generates economic activity that trickles down to help those at the bottom. Before going further, let me summarize the two approaches to fiscal policy so that we have a clear understanding of the difference. Demand-side policy emphasizes government spending as a means of putting money directly into consumers' hands, whereas supply-side policy emphasizes tax cuts for business and upper income individuals, with the idea they will invest more heavily in production.

Both of these approaches aim to reduce the jobless rate. Now, a third approach to stimulating the economy is called monetary policy or monetarism. The leading theorist of monetary policy was economist Milton Friedman, who formulated it at the University of Chicago in the 1950s. Friedman believed fiscal policy was largely ineffective and argued instead that the money supply, the amount of money in circulation, was the key to maintaining a stable economy.

When the economy is weak, he said, the money supply should be increased. With more money in circulation, firms and consumers have more money to invest and spend, thus stimulating both production and spending.

Friedman preferred private control of the money supply, but recognized that the government's Federal Reserve Bank, which is called the Fed for short, had the tools to do the job. And indeed, the Fed has taken on the job. To understand the Fed, we need to recognize that it is not an ordinary bank.

It does not have customers, like our typical bank does. It is a banker's bank. Its members are the national banks and those state banks that qualify and choose to join. To deal with an economic downturn, the Fed can employ a combination of three tools to increase the money supply. One, it can lower the interest rate it charges member banks when they borrow from it.

The lower the rate they pay for their loans, the lower the interest rate they can give to their customers. Cheaper rates stimulate borrowing, which pumps money into the economy; that is, it increases the money supply. The Fed can also increase the amount of money in circulation by lowering what is called the reserve rate. Member banks are required to keep on deposit a certain percentage of their assets. This percentage is the reserve rate.

When the Fed lowers the rate, member banks can loan out more of their assets to customers, thereby putting more money into the economy, helping to stimulate it. Finally, the Fed buys and sells securities, which is a catch-all term for many kinds of investments: bonds, notes, treasury bills, and so on.

During an economic downturn, it can increase its buying level. When it buys a security, it gives money to the seller, which the seller, in turn, can spend or invest, helping to stimulate the economy. Now, each of these approaches-demand-side policy, supply-side policy, and monetary policy, has strengths and weaknesses. Each one also has a political dimension.

To help you understand these aspects, let us look at the most recent major application of each policy approach, starting with supply-side fiscal policy. When Republican George W. Bush took office in 2001, the economy was in recession. That year, and an add-on legislation two years later, Bush persuaded Congress to enact tax cuts that included a decrease in the highest marginal rate on personal income from 39.6% to 35% and a decrease in the capital gains tax, which is the tax on investments, from 20% to 15%. These tax cuts benefited high-income taxpayers, precisely the ones targeted by supply-side policy.

The assumption was that they would invest much of the money, giving the economy a boost. Other taxpayers also got a tax cut. But in dollar terms, it was much smaller.

According to one estimate, the tax savings to Americans in the top 1% of income was more than $50,000 a year or was about $600 a year for those in the middle of the income scale, and less than $100 a year for those in the bottom fifth. In Congress, the vote on the Bush tax cuts divided along party lines, particularly in the 2003 bill. In the House and Senate, over 90% of Republicans supported it and over 90% of Democrats opposed it. Now, why do you think Republicans prefer supply-side fiscal policy? Would you attribute it to their governing philosophy or the nature of their party coalition?

Actually, it is both. Supply-side policy fits their small government philosophy approach because tax cuts do not require a new federal program. Tax cuts are implemented through the tax code. Also, tax cuts on firms and upper incomes go to those who traditionally have sided largely with the Republican Party. Now, what was the effect of the Bush tax cuts? Did they help the economy, as they were intended to do? Economists differ on that question and there is a wide range between the high and low estimates.

The Congressional Budget Office, which has a reputation for being nonpartisan, concluded that the tax cuts had a relatively modest impact on the economy.

Where economists agree is on the effect of the tax cuts on government revenue. Bush, like Reagan before him, argued that the tax cuts would eventually pay for themselves. As the economy strengthened, incomes and profits would rise, and along with that, so would the government's tax revenues. As it turned out, the Bush tax cuts were too large to be paid back later by higher revenues.

According to a study of the National Bureau of Economic Research, the Bush tax cuts added hundreds of billions to the national debt. Now, these assessments have taken some of the luster off supply-side fiscal policy. It has also lost favor because the Bush tax cuts added to the American income divide, the widening gap between the incomes of those at the top of the economic ladder and those at the bottom. Now, let us take a look at recent supply-demand and monetary policy action, which came into play when the economy in 2008 took its sharpest downturn since the Great Depression. Bush was still in the presidency when the downturn began.

He persuaded Congress in early 2008 to enact a tax rebate. It gave $300 per adult and dependent child to taxpayers making less than $75,000 a year, or in the case of a married couple, less than $150,000 a year. This was a demand-side bill because its goal was to put money directly into consumers' hands so that their spending would spur production and job growth. Which members of Congress, Republicans or Democrats, do you think more strongly supported Bush's proposal?

You might have picked Republicans, thinking that they would side with Bush because he was a Republican. In fact, however, congressional Democrats backed the bill more strongly, particularly in the Senate, where every Democrat supported it, while a third of the Republicans were opposed.

Now, why the Democrats? Well, in part because the Democratic Party's coalition tilts toward those of lower income, the main beneficiaries of the tax rebate bill. Upper income taxpayers, who are mostly Republican, were not eligible for the rebate. The 2008 tax rebate cost $150 billion. When President Obama took office in early 2009, an even larger demand side stimulus bill was passed by Congress.

It totaled $787 billion and included for example, more than $100 billion in infrastructure spending, such as road construction and updating the electricity grid; nearly $100 billion in unemployment assistance, such as expanded benefits and training for jobless workers; and more than $100 billion to enable state and local governments to retain their workers and services.

These measures, consistent with demand-side theory, aimed to put money in people's pockets so that they would spend and give the economy a boost. The legislation, as you would expect, had the overwhelming support of Democratic lawmakers. 100%, all of them, of Senate Democrats and over 95% of House Democrats backed it, while no House Republican and only three Senate Republicans supported it.

The legislation fit the Democratic Party's philosophy of using government to promote economic security. It mainly helped those who are part of its coalition: manual workers, government employees, and the marginally employed. In late 2010, the Congressional Budget Office estimated that the stimulus bill increased the number of full-time-equivalent jobs by 2 to 5.2 million compared to what those amounts would have been otherwise. But if the legislation worked as demand-side theory predicted, it added significantly to the federal debt.

The $787 billion tab was paid with borrowed money. That weakened its public support, which proved important when Obama came back to Congress to ask for a second stimulus bill. Republican opposition blocked it. The United States is likely at a point where fiscal policy, whether on the demand or supply side, is not a realistic option if another economic downturn should occur in the near future.

The national debt is now more than $18 trillion, up from less than $6 trillion when Bush took office in 2001. Likely, the votes in Congress do not exist for either a massive federal spending bill or a large tax cut bill, especially since Republicans and Democrats do not see eye to eye on these matters. Infrastructure spending could be an exception.

In his first speech to Congress, President Trump proposed a $1 trillion infrastructure spending bill, saying that our bridges, roadways, and other transportation systems are crumbling and in need of repair, a judgment shared by transportation experts. Infrastructure improvement could be an area where Republicans and Democrats can agree, given that it helps both business and workers. So, let us see how the Federal Reserve responded to the economic downturn of 2008. The Fed quickly discovered that one of its tools, the reserve rate, was not going to be of much help.

Demand for bank loans was weak and banks had lots of cash on hand. So, lowering the reserve rate, allowing banks to loan out a larger share of their assets, was not going to work. On the other hand, in order to stimulate demand for loans, the Fed rapidly dropped the interest rate it charged member banks for their loans.

The rate had been about 5% when signs of trouble in the housing market had first appeared. And by 2009, the rate had dropped to 1%. It would soon go to 1/4 of 1%, basically free loans to member banks. The Fed was also buying securities at a fast clip. The effect was to put money into the hands of sellers, with the hope they would use it in ways that would stimulate economic growth.

By 2009, however, the Fed was running out of options. It had dropped interest rates to near 0%. Nothing more could be done on that front. Subsequently, the Fed resorted to what is called quantitative easing, a tool of last resort. It began to purchase the assets of member banks, such as their mortgage-backed securities.

The goal was to take risky securities off their hands in return for money that they could loan to firms and consumers, and at historically low rates. Now, where did the Fed come up with the money to purchase those bank assets?

For all practical purposes, the Fed created the money out of thin air. The Fed is the nation's central bank and essentially has the power to print money and keep printing it. That is what it did from 2009 until it stopped in 2014. Never in the country's history had so much money been pumped into the economy. All told, the Fed spent more than $3 trillion on quantitative easing.

To give you a sense of how much money that is, it happens to be more money than is generated in a full year by the economy of any country on Earth except the United States, China, Japan, or Germany. Economists' estimates of the effect of the Fed's efforts to stimulate the economy vary widely.

But all concede that the Fed, more than any other institution, contributed to the economic recovery that took place after 2008. But that is not the full story. Monetary policy, the theory, holds that if the money supply is excessive, if there is too much money in circulation, inflation will eventually occur. That is a fear going forward once the US economy gets on a stronger footing. Critics of the Fed's tactics also point out that much of the money the Fed pumped into the economy didn't go into consumers' pockets or production increases, which would have stimulated the economy. Instead, much of it was used by banks and wealthy individuals to play the stock market, which rose sharply because the influx of so much capital.

That widened the income gap in that the average taxpayer doesn't have the means to play the stock market.

A final issue of the Fed relates to how it operates. On one side, admirers of the Fed point out that monetary policy is more flexible than fiscal policy. For instance, the Fed can drop its interest rate on a moment's notice, whereas fiscal policy first requires Congress to act and is then slow in its implementation.

Money for new construction projects, for example, take quite a bit of time to work their way into the economy. The Fed's admirers also like the fact that it is relatively free of the partisan conflict that can hamstring Congress. The Fed's chair and the other six members of its board of governors are nominated by the president and confirmed by Congress. But once chosen, they are largely free to act on their own. Yet to some critics, that is a problem. It means that the Fed is not fully accountable to the people's elected representatives. The critics note that some of its actions are aimed mostly at protecting its member banks. A possible case in point is the loans the Fed gave banks to keep them afloat after the market collapse in 2008. The Fed gave those institutions $7 trillion. That is 10 times the amount Congress gave them through its controversial TARP program. The American public was overly critical of TARP.

They disliked the fact that Congress was bailing out banks while leaving people who were losing their homes to fend for themselves. The public never had a chance to voice its opinion of the Fed's action because it was carried out in secrecy.

When it came to light a few years later, the Fed claimed it acted in secret, so as not to panic world markets about the scale of America's banking crisis. That is no doubt true. But the Fed clearly was protecting its member banks, using public resources to prop them up.

In most democracies, the central bank is subject to greater transparency and greater political control than is the Fed. In some ways, the Fed is not, unlike the federal courts. It operates largely outside the reach of a democratic majority. The justification for that, in the case of the courts, is pretty clear. They need to be independent if they are to protect minority rights. It is less clear why the Fed should have such wide latitude to act on its own. Well, we began by noting that the Great Depression was a watershed in thinking about the government's role in the economy. In that period, Keynesian economics, the idea that government, through its spending, should stimulate consumer demand to help reverse an economic downturn, gained support.

Since then, demand-side fiscal policy, which rests on action by Congress and the president, has been an instrument through which government seeks to manage the economy. It is also significant to note that for reasons of their party philosophy and coalition, Democratic lawmakers are more inclined than Republicans to favor demand-side fiscal policy. Republicans, also for reasons of their party philosophy and coalition, tend to favor supply-side fiscal policy, where government, again, through action by Congress and the president, cuts taxes on firms and upper income taxpayers.

The assumption behind supply-side policy is that with the extra money, moneyed interests will engage in activities that stimulate production, the supply side, which will trickle down into more jobs and consumer spending. The third economic instrument I mentioned earlier is monetary policy, which works through the Federal Reserve.

The Fed has a number of tools-reserve rates, interest rates, the buying and selling of securities and quantitative easing through which to manipulate the money supply. The underlying theory is that, expanding the money supply will stimulate the economy, while shrinking it, will lead to economic contraction. Finally, all three of these mechanisms can be effective, but that none of them is free of criticism or of adverse consequences, or of political controversy.

Regulatory Policy

Regulatory policy is not what most people think of when they look to government for help. It is rare for a regulatory issue to be at the top of the list of what Americans see as the country's most pressing problems. Yet, in terms of its impact on Americans' lives, regulatory action has made a large difference. Automobiles today are much safer than they were a few decades ago as a result of regulations requiring seat belts and airbags. The national highway traffic safety administration estimates that seat belts save 15,000 lives annually, while airbags save an additional 3,000 lives. Cigarettes were once unregulated, but since the 1960s manufacturers have been required by the federal government to place warning labels about the dangers of smoking on cigarette packs. At the state and local government levels bans on smoking in public buildings and accommodations have been widely adopted.

In the 1960s, more than 40 percent of American adults were cigarette smoker; today that number is 20%. As the number has fallen so as the incidence of lung cancer, emphysema, and other smoking related ailments. In 2014, Yale University study has estimated that in the 50 years since the surgeon general's report came out on the adverse consequences of smoking, eight million lives have been saved in the United States through anti-tobacco regulation.

Well how many lives is that?

It is twice the number of everyone currently living in Boston, San Francisco, Seattle, Dallas, Atlanta, and Minneapolis combined. It is more difficult to come up with a reliable estimate of the benefits of the regulatory cleanup of America's air and water. But it is undoubtedly part of the reason that Americans' life expectancy has increased by eight years since the Clean Air and Water Acts were passed in the early 1970s.

That is not to mention the recreational benefits of these laws. Seldom today are Americans told to stay indoors because the air quality is at a dangerous level, or to stay away from the water because it is too polluted for safe swimming, boating, or fishing. I could go on and on about the benefits of regulatory policy. Safer working conditions, minimum wage protections, safer foods and drugs, protection from predatory lenders, the full list would be exceedingly long. There is no question the government regulation can be taken too far. Also, *over-regulation* is not sound policy.

America's problem in the past was *under-regulation.* Fixing that problem has added immeasurably to the quality of Americans' daily lives. As you know, the Boston Harbor, which was once so heavily polluted, it was not fit even for the fishes. That made the harbor an issue of the 1988 presidential campaign, The Republican nominee, George H. W. Bush, accused the Democratic nominee, Massachusetts governor Michael Dukakis, of ignoring the harbor. Bush called it the worst policy mistake in the history of New England. It cost $4 billion to clean up the harbor. Like so many of America's waterways, the Boston Harbor was treated as an open sewer by local businesses.

They dumped the byproducts of their production into the water, including toxic waste. Today, as a result of federal, state, and local regulatory action, the Boston Harbor is fit for the fishes, and also for swimmers and boaters. The goal of regulatory action is to prevent the harmful effects of business practices. Regulation is widespread. The foods that you eat, the drugs you take, the car that you drive and its safety features, all of those things and more are subject to regulatory action.

No one today would argue that we should go back to the era of anything goes. The Boston Harbor is a reminder of that. But at the same time, the question of how far regulation should extend is an open question. But regulation imposes costs on business, and they get passed along to consumers. And that makes regulatory policy a political issue. In this section, we will look at the politics and policies of regulatory action, focusing on some of the harmful business practices it addresses.

Let's look at restraint of trade, which refers to anti-competitive business practices; inequity, which refers to unfair business transactions; moral hazard, which occurs when one party engages in risky economic behavior but then passes the risk onto another party; and negative externalities, which result when firms fail to pay the full costs of their production activity. Now, although regulatory decisions have the appearance of being based solely on economic considerations, they often have a partisan element. The heads of regulatory agencies are nominated by the president and confirmed by the Senate, and the appointees typically share the president's policy priorities. Republican appointees, consistent with their party's ideology, are normally more pro-business than our democratic appointees.

A case in point is Scott Pruitt, who was picked by Donald Trump to head the Environmental Protection Agency and immediately began to weaken some of the standards governing air and water pollution, saying they placed an unreasonable burden on business.

A central concept of economic theory is efficiency. Efficiency refers to the relationship between economic output, what's produced, and economic input, what goes into producing those goods and services. A high level of efficiency is preferable to a low level. It means that society is getting more goods and services out of the same amount of production resources.

Now, our free market promotes efficiency through competition. To compete with other sellers, a firm will try to use as few resources as possible when producing its products in order to keep the price low. Less efficient firms will be forced to become more efficient to cut their production costs in order to remain competitive on pricing. But what happens when competition weakens or dries up? What happens when a producer acquires a monopoly or near monopoly on a product? Well, in that case, they can sell the product at whatever price the market will bear. It does not have to worry about efficiency.

It has a lock on the market. That situation is known as restraint of trade and is a basis for regulatory action. The most famous of such actions was the breakup in the early 1900s of Standard Oil, owned by John D. Rockefeller, the world's richest man. Standard Oil, at one point, controlled 90% of US oil production, allowing it to set prices. In 1911, the Supreme Court, citing the Sherman Antitrust Act of 1890, ordered the breakup of Standard Oil into 33 smaller companies as a means of fostering competition in the oil industry. Today, the primary responsibility for maintaining competitiveness rests with the Federal Trade Commission.

In recent years, for example, the FTC has blocked several proposed hospital mergers on grounds they would deprive local patients of a choice among hospitals, resulting in higher charges for hospital care. That same logic led the FTC in 2016 to block a proposed merger between Staples and Office Depot. The FTC concluded that the merger would create a monopoly in the office supply business in many communities. Equity considerations are another justification for regulatory action. An economic transaction is ordinarily considered equitable if each party enters into it freely and ethically. For example, if a seller knows that a product is defective, equity requires that the buyer also know of the defect.

Sellers do not always behave ethically. They may try to hide a product's defect from potential buyers. A recent example is automobile airbags. Their manufacturer, Takata Corporation, discovered nearly a decade ago that its airbags had a defect that could kill or injure a passenger when the bag inflated. Takata chose not to mention the defect when filing its periodic reports with the National Highway Transportation Agency, the federal agency charged with regulating car safety. When the NHTSA finally became aware of the defect, it used its regulatory authority in 2014 to issue a recall, starting in states with high levels of humidity where the risk of death or injury from the defective airbags is highest. Now, when Congress establishes a regulatory agency, such as the NHTSA, it charges it with protecting the public.

That is the agency's mandate. The NHTSA, in ordering the airbag recall, was fulfilling its mandate. However, regulatory agencies do not always vigorously pursue their public responsibility. They sometimes side with the industry they are supposed to regulate, a situation that scholars describe as agency capture. Agency capture can result from the fact that regulators work closely with the firms they regulate and rely on them for much of the information that goes into their decisions.

An example of agency capture is the Food and Drug Administration's handling of Vioxx, a pain relief drug for people with arthritis and other forms of chronic or acute pain. The drug's manufacturer, Merck Pharmaceuticals, spent hundreds of millions of dollars developing Vioxx. When preliminary tests showed the drug effective at reducing pain, Merck convinced the FDA to clear it for market even though the testing had not been totally thorough. When Vioxx hit the market in 1999, it was an instant success.

It attracted tens of millions of users and generated $2 and 1/2 billion a year in sales for Merck. The problem was that Vioxx was unsafe. Users suffered an abnormally large number of heart attacks and strokes. And five years after its introduction, Vioxx was pulled from the market. Merck eventually paid more than $5 billion in legal claims to Vioxx's victims and their families. A review panel of the US Institute of Medicine concluded that the FDA's testing process had been slanted in Merck's favor and that the FDA had failed to demonstrate accountability to the public. Two years later, Congress passed legislation requiring the FDA to strengthen its pre- and post-marketing testing procedures. Now, a third justification for regulation is what is called moral hazard.

In economics, moral hazard occurs when the risk of a transaction is later transferred to another party. Economist Paul Krugman pointedly describes moral hazard as the situation in which "one person makes the decision about how much risk to take, while someone else bears the cost if things go badly." An example is auto insurance. Some drivers take greater risks, such as driving on icy streets, than they would if they didn't have insurance, knowing that the costs of an accident will be borne by their insurance company. The term "moral hazard" dates to the 17th century, where it described fraudulent or immoral economic transactions, which accounts for the word "moral" being part of the term. Few recent developments illustrate moral hazard more clearly than the subprime home mortgages that helped trigger the near collapse of the American financial sector in 2008.

More than a decade earlier, financial regulations had been relaxed to allow banks to grant mortgages to a wider range of borrowers. Banks jumped at the chance, granting mortgages to poorly qualified homebuyers. By 2006, a third of mortgages were being given to people with weak or unsubstantiated credit. The banks knew that many of the borrowers would not be able to keep up with their payments, so, they sold the mortgages, shifting the risk of default from themselves to unsuspecting buyers. It put the entire housing industry at risk if home prices suddenly dropped, which they did, precipitating the financial crisis of 2008.

Now, if banks had been required to keep many of these mortgages, they would not have risked writing so many bad ones. Banks relieved themselves of the risk by shifting it to those who purchased their mortgages. There was also a second moral hazard at play in the 2008 financial crisis, what has come to be known as the "too big to fail" problem. When the financial system went into a tailspin, Congress and the Federal Reserve stepped in with several trillion dollars in loans to keep large financial institutions, such as bank of America, Citibank, and JPMorgan Chase, from going bankrupt, which would have worsened the financial crisis.

They were too big to fail. If they had gone down, they would have taken the entire economy with them. Yet, it was their risky investment strategies that had put them on the verge of bankruptcy. They had leveraged their assets at roughly 30 to 1, up from the previous level of 12 to 1, in an effort to make ever more money. But that meant, when the economic downturn started, they didn't have enough assets to cover their losses. So, who paid for the risks they took? Well, not the banks themselves. The government assumed the risk. Congress responded in 2010 with the Dodd-Frank Act, which tightened banking regulations.

Among Dodd-Frank's provisions is a requirement that banks retain a larger share of the mortgages they write, particularly those of higher risk.

Dodd-Frank also specifies that in an economic downturn, government can pump money into the economy for the purpose of providing liquidity to the financial system, but not to aid a failing financial company. Now, as we noted earlier, the Dodd-Frank bill provoked sharp partisan disagreement. Democratic lawmakers wrote the legislation, claiming it would protect against a repeat of what happened in 2008. For their part, Republican lawmakers claimed it placed too many restraints on financial institutions and would inhibit economic growth.

One of Republican Donald Trump's first actions as president was to weaken some provisions of Dodd-Frank. Trump said his aim was not to give financial institutions free rein, but instead to pursue policies that would, quote, "encourage economic growth and job creation."

As Trump's words indicate, the question of regulation is rarely one of whether to regulate fully or not to regulate at all. The question is one of finding the proper balance: enough regulation to protect the public from harmful behavior, but not so much regulation as to stifle economic vitality. Let us look at negative externalities, or as some economists prefer to call them, spillover effects. They are also a justification for regulatory action.

A negative externality results when business firms or consumers fail to pay the full cost of production, as in the case of a company whose industrial waste seeps into a nearby lake or river. The health and cleanup cost of the water pollution, the negative externalities, are borne not by the producer, but by society as a whole. For a long period, air and water pollution were not major policy concerns.

Business was more or less allowed to do as it pleased. Then in the 1960s, pressure started to build for government action. Rachel Carson's book, The Silent Spring, which describes the destructive effects of the pesticide DDT, contributed to the movement. But nothing tipped the scales of public opinion more than a burning river. In 1969, Cleveland's Cuyahoga River, which was so heavily polluted with industrial waste that it bubbled with escaping gases, caught fire. The river became the symbol of business practices that had gotten out of hand. The next year, Congress passed the Clean Air Act, which was backed by Republican and Democratic lawmakers alike. The law regulated the emission of hazardous air pollutants. Soon thereafter, Congress, again on a bipartisan basis, passed the Clean Water Act, which regulated water quality standards. Republican President Richard Nixon proposed creation of a new federal agency to oversee the legislation.

The democratic-controlled Congress agreed, and the EPA, short for the Environmental Protection Agency, was created. These bipartisan initiatives led eventually to dramatic improvements in air and water quality. Pollution levels today are far below their levels of the 1960s, when yellowish gray fog, known as smog, hung over cities like Los Angeles and Chicago, and when bodies of water, like the Potomac River and Lake Erie, were open sewers.

In the past four decades, toxic waste emissions have been cut in half, hundreds of polluted lakes and rivers have been revitalized, and urban air pollution has declined by 60%. Today, the issue of pollution is less that of local problems, such as polluted lakes and rivers, than that of a global problem, climate change. In the 1970s, scientists began to note that the Earth's climate was changing at an accelerated rate. By the 1990s, a scientific consensus had emerged-global warming was taking place, driven largely by carbon-based fuel emissions. Computer models suggested a greenhouse effect.

There was an increased number of carbon particles in the atmosphere, and they were trapping heat rather than allowing it to escape into space. The theory was backed by a range of evidence, including an increase in global temperature levels, rising sea levels, and glacial and polar melting.

When climate change first caught the news media's attention, it was reported strictly from a scientific angle, a perspective that pollsters also applied in their opinion polls. Respondents were asked not whether climate change was happening, but how quickly they thought its impact would be felt. In a 1997 Gallup poll, for example, only 9% of respondents said global warming would never happen, while seven times that number felt the impact would be felt during their lifetime. Soon thereafter, however, the nature of both news coverage and public opinion began to change.

Politics had invaded the issue of climate change. The turning point was the Kyoto conference of 1997, where representatives of the world's nations met in Japan to develop a plan for reducing carbon emissions. Democratic President Bill Clinton signed the resulting agreement, known as the Kyoto Protocol. He was unable, however, to convince the Senate to approve the treaty. The Senate's objection was that the treaty was unfair to developed countries like the United States. The protocol required them to reduce their carbon emissions while not requiring the same of developing countries, like China and India. After Republican President George W. Bush took office in 2001, he rejected the Kyoto agreement out of hand, saying it would weaken the nation's struggling economy. Nevertheless, Bush acknowledged a need to address climate change.

"America's unwillingness to embrace a flawed treaty," Bush said, "should not be read as an abdication of responsibility." Some Republicans, including Arizona Senator John McCain, criticized Bush for not showing leadership on climate change. But a larger group of Republican lawmakers, backed by industry lobbyists and conservative talk show hosts, attacked the science itself, arguing that the evidence of climate change was inconclusive or flat out wrong. For the news media, the partisan argument was too good a story to ignore.

The issue shifted from the science pages to the front pages and was played as a "he said, she said" debate. Rather than sorting through the facts behind the opposing claims, the media played up the fight. A research study found that conservative politicians, industry-funded think tanks and other sources that claim climate change was inconsequential or scientifically unproven received the same level of news coverage in the mainstream press during the 1998 to 2002 period as did sources whose views were aligned with the scientific consensus. The debate intensified with the release of the film An Inconvenient Truth. Featuring Clinton's vice president, Al Gore, the film told of the dangers of climate change.

The film received the 2006 Academy Award for documentary film and helped Gore win the 2007 Nobel Peace Prize. For proponents of climate change policy, the film was pure gospel. For some opponents, it was pure propaganda. Said Oklahoma Republican Senator James Inhofe, "If you say the same lie over and over again, people will believe it." A study of Fox News and MSNBC, the conservative and liberal cable TV networks respectively, reveal just how differently climate change was being portrayed by the opposing sides. On Fox, there were three times as many stories dismissive of the climate change thesis as there were supportive stories.

On MSNBC, supportive stories were nearly the only ones aired. As for the mainstream media, the reporting was beginning to tilt toward the scientific consensus, but there were still plenty of coverage of the opposing view, as a study of the coverage in the New York Times and Wall Street Journal revealed. Now, let us take a look at what was happening to public opinion as the climate change issue became increasingly politicized. Republicans and Democrats differed only slightly in their views on global warming before the 1997 Kyoto conference. After Kyoto, they began to diverge, Democrats becoming more accepting of climate change, and Republicans becoming less accepting.

The gap further even widened after the Bush administration rejected the Kyoto protocol, and it widened still further during that period dominated by the Gore film. The gap remains wide even today. In a recent Pew Research Center poll, for example, 79% of Democrats agreed that there is solid evidence the earth has been warming, compared with only 37% of Republicans. We don't have to search hard for an explanation for the difference. Research indicates that when the media play up both sides of partisan debate, citizens tend to pick the side that fits their partisan preference in this instance, Republicans rejecting the climate change thesis, and Democrats embracing it.

That example provides further evidence of the media's contribution to the partisan divide over climate change. As you can see, the US media are much more likely than the media elsewhere to give voice to those who argue against the scientific consensus on global warming. The American press, for example, is twice as likely to do so as is the French press, three times as likely to do so as is the press in India, and 18 times as likely as is the Brazilian press. Now, why do you think the issue of climate change has played out so differently than the environmental issues of the early 1970s when bipartisanship characterized the response?

I think there are quite a few reasons. First, we have talked about frequently in this book, the rise of party polarization. The parties are now so far apart with so few leaders in the middle that it's hard for them to come together to settle their differences.

The second is that climate change touches multiple sectors of the economy. Whereas industrial pollution of waterways, for example, was largely an issue of particular industries, regulation of carbon emissions would affect the transportation sector, the energy sector, the housing sector, and many other sectors. Policy disputes are invariably harder to resolve when a large number of conflicting interests are involved. There is also the fact that the issue is a global one. No country by itself can fix the problem. And a country that takes on the issue, if others aren't, places itself at a competitive disadvantage in global trade because of the added cost of its production.

A final reason is that climate change is hard to see. In the days when smog hung over America's cities and its waterways had the smell of a sewer, pollution was still undeniable. Climate change is invisible by comparison. It is why many doubt its existence or think it's not an urgent issue.

We have made the point in earlier segments of this book that America's system of divided powers is an obstacle to legislative action on large issues. Without a sense of urgency, law-making is often pushed down the road to a later time. Now, before we wrap up this segment, it is imperative to make a general observation about regulatory policy. It is based on the cost and benefits of public policies. The cost and benefits can be concentrated that is, focused on a particular interest or they can be defuse that is, spread across the society.

Let me give you a specific policy to think about, one that many economists have proposed as a response to climate change. It is a tax on carbon. The tax would be levied on carbon emitters as a means of encouraging them to reduce their carbon emissions. As with a carbon tax, most regulatory policy involves concentrated costs and diffuse benefits. A carbon tax would impose costs on particular interests, such as owners of coal-fueled power plants, while the benefits, fewer carbon emissions and less global warming, would be spread across society as a whole.

In such instances, the targeted interest, the one that has paying the cost, will fight hard to block the policy, while the beneficiaries, since the payoff to them is less tangible, won't work is as to support the policy.

This feature of regulatory policy is a reason that elected officials usually prefer to leave regulation decisions in the hands of federal agencies. They can blame the agency for a policy decision rather than having to shoulder the burden themselves. You remember from previous arguments, that elected officials typically prefer policies that provide a concentrated benefit while diffusing the cost. Such policies allow them to take credit with the interest receiving the benefit while largely voiding blame, since the costs to any single taxpayer are hardly noticeable.

Perhaps it will not surprise you, then, that the few policy actions Congress has taken in response to climate change have been of this type as opposed to the regulatory type. President Bush, for example, worked with Congress to pass a bill in 2007 that provided funding for alternative sources of energy. Bush called the bill "a major step toward confronting global climate change." The bill passed by a wide margin, attracting the support of Republican and Democratic lawmakers alike. The bill contained concentrated benefits and diffused costs. The benefits went directly to developers and producers of clean energy, while the costs are spread across the taxpaying public. From the perspective of an elected official, that type of policy is good politics. They can get the credit without having to shoulder the blame.

As argued earlier, regulatory policy aims primarily to reduce the harmful effects of business activity.

One reason why regulation might occur is restraint of trade, the situation where a firm gain or could gain a monopoly or near-monopoly, and thus would be positioned to set prices at an artificially high level. Regulatory action in this case could consist of denying a merger between competing firms or breaking a large firm into a number of smaller, competing firms. Another reason for regulation is inequity, when one party to an economic transaction has an unfair advantage over another party, as when it hides information about a product's defect.

In this case, regulatory action could include requiring the producer to replace the product or to pay damages. Another reason for regulation is what is called moral hazard, the situation where one party takes risks and then passes that risk along to another party. The problem in the context of bank's risky mortgage practices in the period leading up to the 2008 financial crisis.

The regulatory response, in that instance, was Dodd-Frank, which imposes tighter restrictions on financial institutions. Finally, negative externalities, the situation where economic actors do not pay the full cost of their decisions, as when their production activity creates pollution.

So, regulatory action in such instances can require them to pay part or all the costs to correct or reduce the problem they created. In my discussion of negative externalities, I took special note of climate change and the partisan challenge to regulation in that policy area. Regulatory action typically involves concentrated costs, which heightens opposition to regulation by the firms that would have to pay those costs.

Welfare and Income Policy

While wage stagnation has caught the attention of policymakers of both parties: Republican and Democratic lawmakers are hopelessly at odds over taxes, they both acknowledge the need to address the problem of wage stagnation. What might be done to boost the income of the average American?

Let us take a look at education policy, an area targeted by the OECD, which stands for the Organization for Economic Cooperation and Development. The OECD has 34 industrialized countries including the United States as its members. It analyzes economic developments in these countries and offers policy recommendations. In the view of OECD, US education policy is out of step with the demands of today's economy, which rewards those with high skills, but hurts those with low skills or skills that are in low demand.

The OECD is particularly critical of America's early childhood education. Although the United States spends more on primary and secondary education than the average OECD country, it spends significantly less on early childhood education, particularly for those from low- and moderate-income families. This puts affected children from these families at risk when they start school.

They perform less well academically and are less likely to attend college than their peers who received a quality early childhood education. On reaching adulthood, many of these children fall in the low skill category, which for most of them means a lifetime of low income and job insecurity. The OECD also notes the slippage in America's position as the leader in higher education.

At one time, the United States had far and away the world's largest proportion of college graduates. That position has been eroding, even though the income returns from a college degree in the United States exceeds that of most OECD countries. The problem here, as the OECD sees it, is that the cost of college is now much higher in the United States than elsewhere. At one time, government paid the large share of the cost of attending a public college or university, which is where most Americans get a college degree. Increasingly, the cost has been shifted to students in the form of higher tuition. That is had two negative consequences for people's income. One is that the high cost of college has dissuaded some people from attending. Even though there is a long-term income payoff from getting a degree, the upfront short-term cost of paying for college is too high for some high school graduates-- particularly those from lower and middle-income families.

The second consequence is that most students leave college with a substantial loan debt. According to a recent study by the Federal Reserve, college loan debt now exceeds the total of all credit card debts; a consequence is that many young college educated instead of buying homes and cars that would improve their lives and help fuel the economy, are spending a large portion of their income in paying off college debt. These problems, early childhood education, and the cost of a college education, could be improved by government action. And their alleviation would help in the long run to overcome wage stagnation.

The open question is whether US policymakers will take the necessary action. They have taken a first step by acknowledging the need for policy change at the preschool and college levels. The next step, actually doing something on a scale they would make a difference, is the uncertain one. Economic class has not been as big a part of American politics as it has been in Europe. Labor unions have always been weaker here. Only about one in eight American workers belongs to a union That's true even in the construction business behind me. The European average is twice that.

Europe also has a tradition of working-class parties, like the Labor Party in Britain or the Social Democratic Party in Germany. The United States does not have and has never had a major labor or social democratic party.

The reason is the cultural differences between the United States and Europe. Class awareness is much stronger in Europe, which has lent support for labor unions and working-class parties. The United States culture emphasizes individualism, the person making it on his or her own. That is made it harder to get collective action around the workplace. The fact that economic issues are less important in the United States does not mean, however, that they are insignificant. During the 1930s' Great Depression, economic policy was on everybody's mind.

The minimum wage, collective bargaining, those came out of the Great Depression of the 1930s. Today, economic issues are back to the forefront. The economic downturn that began in 2008 cost many Americans their savings and their jobs. And there is not a full recovery yet. Additionally, for the average American worker, wages have been pretty stagnant for the last couple of decades, while at the top, incomes are growing, creating an income gap that is increasingly a political issue. Generational differences are also playing into the economic issue. Some analysts believe that this generation of young adults will be financially less well off than their parents. These developments have made economic issues an increasingly important part of American politics. Class refers to people who share the same economic status.

Some people are well off and are collectively referred to as the upper class or the wealthy. Others make enough money to have a comfortable lifestyle, though not one free of financial worry. They are typically referred to as the middle class. Then, there are those who can make ends meet, but it's a close call, the so-called working class. Finally, there is the lower class or the poor, those that struggle to keep food on the table and a roof over their heads. For most people, financial well-being is chiefly a question of employment what type of job they hold, how secure it is, and how well it pays. But government policies also play a role in how society's financial resources are distributed.

These policies will be the focus in this segment. We will look at the nation's social welfare policies, those that help people meet their basic needs, and its income policies, those that help people get ahead financially. Let us explore several subjects explored in previous policies, including the nation's political culture, its political structure, and its party and group systems. Now, poverty is a large and persistent problem in the U.S. Although the U.S. has less poverty than many countries, it has more poverty than comparable ones. Its poverty level, for example, is twice that of France and Germany. It is also significantly higher than that of Great Britain and also that of our northern neighbor Canada.

The U.S. government uses the cost of living as the basis for divining the poverty line, which is the level of income below which a family is defined as poor and thereby eligible for certain forms of public assistance. The government sets the threshold for poverty as the annual cost of a thrifty food budget multiplied by 3 to cover the cost of housing, clothing, and other necessities. By this indicator, a family of two is judged to be poor if its total income is less than 16,000. Now, that is not a lot of money for two people.

It works out to, about $44 a day. Keep in mind that money has to feed and clothe two people, give them a place to live, provide them transportation, and cover the rest of their expenses. That is a tight budget. $44 a day is only slightly more than what the average college student pays for room and board. That is for only one person and just for food and shelter. By the government's formula, about one in seven Americans live in poverty. That is roughly 45 million people. If they could somehow join hands and form a line, it would stretch all the way from New York City to Los Angeles and then back again. That is a lot of people.

America's poor include individuals of all ages, races, and regions. But it is concentrated among certain groups. Minority group members have a poverty rate twice that of whites. Women have a poverty rate exceeding that of men. Children are one of America's most impoverished groups.

Roughly one in five American children live in poverty, most of them in a single parent family headed by the mother. Now, until the 1930s' Great Depression, state governments had responsibility for the poor. Welfare was among the policy areas deemed reserved to the states by the 10th Amendment. That doctrine changed as a result of the Depression, a period when one in four workers couldn't find a job and another one in four had only part-time work.

Income fell sharply. And as it did, so did state tax revenues. Most states were too broke to help their poor. Federal tax revenues had also declined. But unlike the states, a point we made earlier, the federal government has unlimited power to print and borrow money. During the Depression, the federal government was in the hands of officials, President Franklin Roosevelt, and a Democratic Congressional majority that had no qualms about using the federal government's spending power to help the poor.

Most Depression era poverty programs were meant to be temporary, such as the Works Projects Administration, which put millions of Americans to work constructing roads, public hospitals, and the like. But a few programs were designed to last, including the Aid for Dependent Children program, which was later renamed the Aid for Families with Dependent Children program or AFDC. It provided financial assistance to poor single mothers, those who had little or no income by reason of the father's death or desertion.

A second wave of anti-poverty programs came in the 1960s, when the federal government was again in the hands of a President, Lyndon Johnson, and a Democratic Congress determined to help the poor. They enacted the largest set of anti-poverty programs in the nation's history, including the food stamps program, subsidized housing, and Medicaid, which is government-paid health insurance for those of low income. These programs had the public support. The Gallup poll at the time found that 2/3 of Americans believe that government has a responsibility to try to do away with poverty in this country. The programs also had an element of bipartisan support.

Republican lawmakers from New England and the upper Midwest states of Minnesota and Wisconsin, the strongholds of the party's progressive tradition, strongly backed the new programs.

In the House vote on the Medicaid bill, for example, 90% of progressive state Republicans supported it. That period was the high watermark of the government's anti-poverty efforts. Since then, there have been only a few new programs, including the 2010 Affordable Care Act, which among its provisions expands Medicaid eligibility and provides subsidized health insurance to lower income families. There have also been cutbacks, most notably the 1996 Welfare Reform Act, which reduced the welfare rolls by changing the rules.

As you will recall, the 1996 legislation eliminated the FDC program, which had placed no limit on how long a family could receive benefits. In its stead, the 1996 law created the TANF program, which limits eligibility for most families to five years. Now, programs such as food stamps and Medicaid are public assistance programs.

They are labeled as such, because they are funded with general tax revenues, and they are available only to the financially needy. Public assistance programs are means tested. Recipients must prove they are poor in order to qualify for the benefit, a requirement that adds to the program's expense. In addition to payments to recipients, there are administrative costs associated with determining whether an applicant's income falls below the designated amount. These costs account for about 10% of federal spending on food stamps and about 5% on Medicaid. Means testing is consistent with America's culture of individualism, the belief that people should be self-reliant.

That belief supports the notion that public assistance should be available only to those who can prove that they are unable to make it on their own. The distinctiveness of the American approach can be seen by comparing the US health care system with many of those in Europe. In those cases, residents of all income levels are entitled to government paid medical care.

If they become ill, they simply go to a clinic or hospital for treatment at government expense, no questions asked. In contrast, Americans receive government paid health care only if they meet the eligibility criteria. Even then, to be eligible, they must apply beforehand for insurance and prove that they are too poor to buy it on their own. There is another feature of the American welfare system that is distinctive. Consider, for example, the difference in the monthly assistance payments to poor families depending on where they live. The payments range from less than $300 a month to $500 a month and more.

So, what explains the difference?

Do you think it is because the locations differ in their cost of living or because the locations are in different states?

It is the second one. Because of America's federal system, most public assistance programs, although funded primarily by the federal government, are administered by the states, which have a degree of control over benefits and eligibility. As this map shows, there is considerable variation in the amount of family assistance that states provide. Some states provide more than $500 a month, while some provide less than half as much. The average across all the states is roughly $400, but the range is wide. Now, public assistance programs are not America's only social welfare policies.

These policies also include what are called social insurance programs. As the name implies, they are based on the insurance principle. Individuals must pay into the program in order to receive the benefits. Social security is the leading social insurance program. Established in the 1930s as part of Franklin Roosevelt's New Deal, it provides monthly social security benefits to retirees who paid social security tax on their income while working. The current tax rate is 6.2%.

That amount is deducted on payday from workers' wages. Social security is an entitlement program. This means that if an individual meets the eligibility requirement, he or she is entitled to the designated benefit. Government cannot decide one day to cancel an entitlement program or to grant the benefit to some previously eligible recipients while denying it to others. Public assistance programs do not offer this type of protection.

They are not entitlement programs. The poor do not have an unqualified claim to benefits. Government can choose at will to cancel such a program or change its eligibility criteria, as in the case of TANF, which reduced the length of time a family can receive public assistance.

Now, in Medicaid, health care for the poor was enacted in 1965. Congress also enacted Medicare, which is health care for retirees. Unlike Medicaid, which is a public assistance program, Medicare is a social insurance program. As is the case with social security, it is financed by a special tax, currently 1.45% on workers' wages. Social security and Medicare are federal programs in their entirety. States do not administer them or have a say in eligibility or benefits. Accordingly, recipients get the same level of benefits regardless of where they reside. Social security and Medicare are highly efficient programs in that they do not require a large bureaucracy to check and recheck recipients' eligibility.

When workers reach the prescribed age and conditions of eligibility, they automatically qualify for the benefits. Less than 1% of social security spending is eaten up by administrative costs. Medicare is more administratively complex in that it involves payments to doctors and hospitals. Even so, according to a Kaiser Family Foundation study, only about 2% of Medicare spending is for expenses other than patient care. In contrast, some private insurance companies, which seek to make a profit and heavily market their products, spend up to 20%, 10 times the amount for Medicare, on non-patient care. Now, Social Security and Medicare are not poverty programs in the literal sense.

Recipients actually come from all income groups.

In fact, the higher one's income while working, the larger the social security payment upon retirement. Such individuals pay more in Social Security taxes during their working years and accordingly get a larger benefit when they retire. The average monthly benefit is about $1,200. But some recipients get less than 1,000, whereas others get more than 2,500. As it happens, families in the top fifth by income receive more in Social Security and Medicare benefits than the poor receive in total on food stamps, housing, and dependent care. Nevertheless, Social Security helps to keep millions of Americans out of poverty.

About one fourth of America's elderly have no significant monthly income aside from what they receive from Social Security. Public assistance and social insurance programs differ, as you might expect, in their level of public support. Polls indicate that most Americans are convinced that Social Security, a social insurance program, is worth the cost. Only a small percentage think that too much is spent on Social Security. Americans have a much less favorable view of public assistance programs. A large number of Americans think that government spends too much on these programs.

The difference reflects America's cultural values. Social insurance programs are funded by special payroll taxes on workers and in that sense are widely seen as something that recipients have earned.

In contrast, public assistance programs are widely seen as handouts, needed by some, but abused by others who are too lazy to get a job. A recent Pew Research Center poll found, for example, that roughly half the public thinks the poor have easy lives, because they get government benefits, they do not work for. This view makes public assistance programs a political target. They have been caught up in the heightened party polarization.

In the Pew survey I just mentioned, Republicans were more than twice as likely as Democrats to say that the poor have easy lives. More than 60% of Republicans held that belief, compared with less than 30% of Democrats. The partisan gap is at least as wide among lawmakers. In 2014, for instance, Congressional Republicans sought a $40 billion reduction in the food stamp program, settling for an $8 billion cut after a threatened veto by Democratic President Barack Obama. Social Security, on the other hand, has withstood partisan challenges. In 2005, President George W Bush proposed to partially privatize social security.

Workers would have had the chance of putting a portion of their Social Security tax payments into a personal retirement account. Bush was forced to back down in the face of strong resistance from senior citizens spearheaded by the AARP, a senior's group that is one of Washington's most powerful lobbies.

On the other hand, poverty lobbies, groups that petition Congress on behalf of the poor, are relatively weak. As you can see in this chart, spending on Social Security has risen dramatically in recent years, while spending on TANF assistance to poor families has declined. Public assistance programs like TANF are vulnerable to cultural and partisan forces to a degree that social insurance programs are not. Let me provide a final example of how cultural values affect poverty policy. Poll after poll over the past 50 years has found that Americans, consistent with their cultural beliefs, see jobs rather than public assistance as the answer to poverty. Not surprisingly, that principle is the basis for some federal poverty programs. The work requirement of the TANF program is one example. Another is EITC, which is shorthand for the Earned Income Tax Credit.

EITC was created in 1975, when Republican Gerald Ford was in the White House and Democrats controlled Congress. EITC provides a refundable tax credit to low income workers. If your job pays low wages, below about 15,000 a year if you are single, you get the credit, with the amount varying by family size and earnings. The average recipient gets a refund of about $2,500, which is obtained when filing one's annual tax return. EITC is a reward for working, a program that is in line with America's cultural values. Now, let us shift the focus to income policy, government policies that affect people's livelihoods.

Until the 1930s' Great Depression, the federal government openly sided with business in its dealings with workers. Efforts to organize unions and improve working conditions were repeatedly blunted by government policy. That changed in the 1930s. Congressional Democrats had their largest majority in a century and enacted pro-labor legislation that included a minimum wage law and collective bargaining rights. Congress also made the personal income tax more progressive, meaning that the tax rate was increased for higher incomes. The top rate was set at a high level, 79% on income above $5 million. Corporate executives claimed that such policies would ruin the nation's economy. But between 1950 and 1970, the economy grew at an unprecedented rate. With that, workers' incomes rose at a record pace, spawning an ever-larger middle class. This economic boom was fueled in part by the strength of America's manufacturing sector. The United States was far and away the world's leading manufacturer.

The US had emerged from World War II with its factories intact, whereas those in other major industrial nations had been damaged by the war. It was a boon for America's factory workers. The best paying factory jobs were those held by union workers. Armed with collective bargaining rights, they were able to secure high wages and, in some cases, health insurance. Union jobs propelled millions of families into the middle class. At peak in the 1950s, a third of America's workers were unionized.

Depending on occupation, they had incomes 10% to 30% higher than their non-union counterparts. The minimum wage was also a contributing factor, particularly for unskilled workers. It put a floor on their income and had the added effect of pushing up the hourly pay of others. Equally dramatic was the impact of the GI Bill, which Congress had enacted near the end of World War II. It gave military veterans cash payments for college and vocational training and provided nearly interest free loans for home purchases and small business ventures.

Before the GI Bill, college and home ownership were out of reach for most families. By the time the original GI Bill expired in the mid '50s, nearly 8 million veterans had participated in its education benefits, 2 and 1/2 million had acquired a home loan, and hundreds of thousands had received small business and farm loans. The impact was felt from Wall Street to Main Street. However, the upward momentum did not last. Since 1970, as this chart shows, most Americans have seen almost no growth in real income, which is income adjusted for inflation. As you can see, the bottom quintile, next to the bottom quintile, and middle quintile of wage earners are no better off today than they were back in 1970, nearly a half a century ago.

In other words, the wages of the bottom 60% of workers have been flat year after year. In terms of real income, their pay has stagnated. As you can also see from the chart, the top two quintiles have enjoyed wage growth. For the next to top quintile, income in real dollars has gone from about $60,000 on average in 1970 to roughly $80,000 today. The top quintile has done even better. Their income has risen over four decades from about $100,000 a year on average to roughly $180,000 a year today. But the biggest winners have been those at the very top, as this chart indicates. Since 1970, the percentage of all national income received by the top 1% of earners has jumped from roughly 10% to roughly 20%. In other words, their real income has doubled, such that the top 1% now gets roughly one in five of all dollars earned by American workers.

The median yearly income for this group exceeds $600,000. The mean exceeds a million. Here is a chart that puts that amount in historical perspective. As you can see, the top 1% are now positioned where they were at the end of the 1920s, the so-called Roaring '20s. After the 1920s, the era when the minimum wage, collective bargaining, and a steeply progressive income tax were in full force, the top 1% saw their share of income decline substantially. But in the past four decades, they have climbed back to that earlier point. What explains this development? Why is the income of most Americans stagnated, while that of top earners has shot up, resulting in a high level of income inequality?

Commentators regularly link the two, as if income gains at the top are the main reason for income stagnation at the bottom. But, in fact, the two developments are only loosely related. The explanation for why top earners has done so well owes substantially to changes in public policy. In contrast, the explanation for wage stagnation owes chiefly to changes in the structure of the nation's economy. Let us look at both of these explanations, starting with the role of public policy in fueling income growth at the top.

As you will recall from our previous discussion of the supply side fiscal policies of Ronald Reagan and George W Bush, the assumption underlying these policies is that reduction in taxes on business and high-income taxpayers will stimulate economic growth. However, the direct effect of the supply side policies was a cut in taxes for high earners. Other public policies have also contributed to the income gap. Reductions in capital gains taxes have overwhelmingly favored the wealthy. They own the large share of stocks, the gains from which are taxed at a much lower rate than the tax on wages. Financial deregulation and trade agreements, which we will look at later, have also disproportionately worked to the benefit of high earners. I could provide other examples too, but the point would be the same. America's wealthy have benefited substantially from the public policies of recent decades. Now, changes in policy do not fully explain income gains at the top.

Global economic change has also worked in favor of those with upper incomes, not only in the United States, but elsewhere as well. But as this chart shows, America's top 1% has fared much better than the top 1% in comparable countries, where government policy is not tilted so heavily in favor of upper incomes. The wealthy's income gains in the United States have not, however, at least in a direct way, come at the expense of lower wage earners. The Bush tax cuts for the wealthy were not achieved by increasing the tax burden on others. All income categories realized a tax savings from the Bush tax cuts during the nine-year period from 2004 to 2012 that they were in full effect. But what stands out most clearly in the figure is the distribution of the tax cuts. For those in the bottom 20%, the total gain over the nine years was less than $1,500. For middle income households, the savings was roughly $10,000. On the other hand, the top 1% on average saved more than $500,000 on their taxes during those nine years. So, who paid for the tax cuts?

The cuts were financed through borrowing, which means the cost was shifted to future generations. The Congressional Budget Office estimates that the Bush tax cuts added about $1.6 trillion to the national debt, not including interest on the borrowing. The sharp increase in wealth among the richest Americans has made tax policy a top issue. The public as a whole, as this chart shows, thinks upper income individuals pay too few taxes.

But there is a large difference of opinion between Democrats and Republicans on the issue. A large majority of Democrats think upper income individuals pay too few taxes, while most Republicans think otherwise. The difference is even more pronounced among lawmakers. Congressional Democrats have repeatedly pressed for increased taxes on the wealthy, opposed at each step by Republican lawmakers.

Democrats have framed their argument in terms of fairness, while Republicans have framed their argument in terms of economic growth. Neither side has shown any willingness to compromise.

In 2011, for example, a Congressional deadlock over taxing and spending nearly led the US for the first time in its history to default on its debt obligations. Now, let us turn to the problem of stagnant wages. As I indicated, the story here is mostly one of changes in the US economy. The manufacturing sector economy that America had after World War II, with its well-paying factory jobs, has given way to a service sector economy. Until 1970, the United States, was a net exporter. Manufacturing goods made in America were being sold around the world. Since then, the United States has been a net importer, buying more goods from abroad than it is selling abroad. Millions of well-paying factory jobs have been lost in the process.

That loss has been accompanied by a sharp decline in union membership. Today, only about one in eight workers is a union member. And most of them work not in the private sector, but in the public sector, such as teachers, police, and civil servants. Less than 10% of private sector workers today are unionized. The economist Lawrence Mitchell has estimated that as much as a third of the wage erosion among some categories of workers owes to the decline of private sector union membership. Since the 1970s, job growth has been in the service sector, area such as banking, rental services, health care, entertainment, fast food, housekeeping.

Service sector employees are difficult for unions to organize, because they work closely with managers and often in small offices. Now, some service sector workers do fairly well financially. Those working for large businesses have salaries on average that are even slightly higher than those working at manufacturing jobs. But there is a wide range of service sector workers, such as waiters, store clerks, hotel staff, artists, lower level administrators, taxi drivers that take home substantially less pay than their factory counterparts. It is also the case that service sector jobs generate less economic activity than do factory jobs. Jobs generate jobs.

That is a basic axiom of economics.

Those who work at restaurants, for example, support jobs for workers in firms that supply food and drink to restaurants. Over the course of a year, the average service sector worker generates nearly $100,000 in related economic activity. Now, that might seem like a lot, but it is substantially less than the average for manufacturing jobs. That figure is closer to $300,000. Consider auto workers.

When new cars leave the factory, they generate lots of economic activity. They support car dealerships, gas stations, repair shops, auto parts makers, auto supply stores, and more. Factory jobs have a much larger job multiplier than do service jobs. America's transition from a manufacturing economy to a service sector economy is due mostly to economic factors. The US dominated global market that existed after World War II has given way to a highly competitive global market, where US firms must compete with those of Japan, Germany, Korea, China, and other countries, some of which have the comparative advantage of paying lower wages. Where public policy fits into the story of wage stagnation is largely a story of what government has not done. The erosion in the value of the federal minimum wage is an example. Today, adjusted for inflation, the minimum wage is about 25% below its peak value in the late 1960s.

Congress establishes the minimum wage level, and lawmakers have not increased it enough to keep up with inflation. Government has also shied from initiatives that could boost employment and wages. In the 1930s through 1960s, government was active in job creation on a large scale. It launched a wide range of infrastructure projects, everything from the Tennessee Valley Authority to the Interstate Highway System. The latter, initiated in 1956 at the urging of Republican President Dwight D Eisenhower, resulted in the construction of 41,000 miles of multi-lane highway, which generated hundreds of thousands of construction and construction-related jobs, not to mention the jobs created by the thousands of roadside businesses that sprung up alongside the interstate. Is there such a role for government today?

There is, at least in the view of the American Society of Civil Engineers. In 2013, it conducted a massive study of the condition of America's infrastructure, its highways, dams, schools, and other public facilities. Using a standard A to F grading scale, the society gave the United States an overall grade point average of D plus, concluding that $3.6 trillion in infrastructure spending is needed by 2020. How likely is it that the government will take on the task of repairing the nation's infrastructure? The odds increased when President Trump in his first speech to Congress proposed a $1 trillion infrastructure bill.

If such a bill had been proposed by a Democratic president, it would not have had a chance of getting through the Republican controlled Congress. But given Trump's backing of the bill and the fact that they could shape the bill to reflect their priorities, Republican lawmakers might be persuaded to back it.

Poverty is a large and persistent problem in the United States, affecting about one in seven Americans. The federal government has a range of policies aimed at alleviating poverty, including food stamps, Medicaid, and assistance to families with dependent children. These are public assistance programs that are means tested, available only to those that can prove they need them, a process consistent with America's culture of self-reliance. Social welfare policy also includes social insurance programs, such as social security.

Recipients qualify for the benefits such programs offer by paying special taxes on their wages when working. This feature has given them a level of public and political support higher than that of public assistance programs. We then turned to income policy, starting with policies such as the minimum wage, collective bargaining, and the GI Bill that contributed to the sharp growth in personal income at all levels after World War II.

We then noted the flattening of income since 1970s for most Americans, a development accompanied by a sharp rise in income at the top of the income ladder, trends that have resulted in a huge income gap between the wealthy and the rest of American society. We explained that these two developments, more wealth at the top and stagnation elsewhere, owe to largely different factors. Public policies in recent decades, including tax policy, have contributed significantly to wealth accumulation at the top of the income ladder. On the other hand, wage stagnation is explained mostly by changes in the American economy and particularly by the transition from a manufacturing-based economy to a service-based economy.

U.S. Foreign Policy

Beyond the positive aspects of trade in foreign policy, there is also a negative application, the imposition of economic sanctions on a country if it behaves badly.

As US Ambassador Richard Holbrooke once said, "Economic sanctions are the policy option that falls somewhere between empty rhetoric on the one hand and going to war on the other. Sanctions are more than mere words, but less than military action." Now economic sanctions do not apply to all conflict situations. They would not work against terrorist groups like ISIS or Al Qaeda because they do not have formal institutional or economic systems that can be targeted and weakened through sanctions. But sanctions are an option when a nation violates international norms or threatens the security of others.

A case in point is the sanctions that the United States and its European allies recently levied on Russia in response to its takeover of the Crimea, which is part of the Ukraine, and for supporting Russian separatists in eastern Ukraine. The sanctions included freezes on the financial assets of wealthy Russians with close ties to Russian President Vladimir Putin. In recent years North Korea and Iran have also been targeted with economic sanctions in an attempt to get them to halt their nuclear weapons programs.

Now, do sanctions work? Do they get a targeted nation to change its behavior? The answer appears to be only sometimes. Sanctions can clearly hurt a nation's economy. After sanctions were imposed on Russia, the value of its currency, the ruble, fell sharply, as did its stock market, while its economic growth turned negative. Sanctions can also hurt a targeted nation's people.

During the more than two decades North Korea has been under US sanctions, its poverty rate has risen sharply, and its life expectancy level has fallen. But do sanctions get nations to change their behavior? Studies by David Alexian and others indicate that though sanctions occasionally succeed, they usually do not. Case in point is Cuba. The United States imposed sanctions on Cuba in 1960 following its nationalization of American-owned firms on the island.

US companies were barred from doing business with Cuba, and travel to and from Cuba was restricted. The sanctions did not get Cuba to alter its policies. And in 2014, President Obama moved to restore relations with Cuba. Said Obama, "These 50 years have shown that isolation has not worked." Now why are sanctions ineffective in most cases? Well, one reason is that top leaders of a targeted country rarely suffer personal hardship from the sanctions. They can also turn the sanctions to their political advantage.

Putin's popularity rose after he told Russians that the United States was trying, through sanctions, to destroy Russia. The effect of sanctions can also be undercut by the actions of other countries. When the United States and its Western allies-imposed sanctions on Iran, China increased its trade with Iran. Then, too, economic sanctions can fail because they are not strong enough.

Sanctioning nations typically stop short of imposing measures that will hurt themselves as well. The Russian sanctions, for example, did not shut the Russian economy off from the international banking system. That action would have hurt European countries that depend on Russia for trade and for its natural gas and oil. Despite such limitations, sanctions have become the preferred alternative to war as an instrument of foreign policy. As Jeremy Greenstock, former British Ambassador to the United Nations noted, "Military action is increasingly unpopular, and in many ways ineffective, and words alone don't work.

So, something in between these is necessary. What else is there besides sanctions?" When Americans think of national security they tend to think in terms of military threats. But national security is also a question of maintaining a nation's way of life, whether people have the jobs and the goods that they are accustomed to.

Increasingly we have asked that question in the context of international trade. Many of the goods that we buy come from abroad. Each day about 6 million containers arrive in the United States from other countries carrying everything from television sets, to clothes, to toys, you name it. That globalized economy has turned out to be both a challenge and an opportunity for the United States. The United States has important comparative advantages.

We have a vibrant tech sector. And we have the most fertile agricultural sector in the world. Those two sectors through international trade have generated millions of American jobs. But we also have comparative disadvantages. The wage scale in the United States is much higher than it is in countries like China, and India, and Guatemala. That means that those goods often can be produced more cheaply abroad. That is good for consumers. We pay less for the goods we buy, as a result. But it also means that millions of American jobs have been lost to foreign firms.

The fact that global trade involves winners and losers has made it one of the most important policy issues of our time. US foreign policy is rooted in what is called, the national interest, the conditions necessary to protect American security and well-being.

President Dwight D. Eisenhower described the national interest as well as anyone. Said Eisenhower, "We do not keep security establishments merely to defend property, or territory, or rights abroad, or at sea. We keep the security forces to defend a way of life." In previous segments, we discussed how diplomacy and national defense fit into America's foreign policy.

Here we will concentrate on foreign trade, examining American's emergence as a global economic power, the connection between trade and national security, and the emergence of free trade as a cornerstone of contemporary US foreign policy. At the end of WWI, the United States was the world's strongest military power and its strongest economic power. Large parts of Europe and Asia had been devastated by the war.

Whereas America's manufacturing sectors were intact. The US economy was generating half of all the world's goods and services, and the American dollar had replaced the British pound as the leading international currency. The United States took the lead role in rebuilding Western Europe and Japan. The most ambitious effort was the Marshall Plan, which provided more than $150 billion, in today's dollars, for European reconstruction. When the Marshall Plan concluded in 1952 the economy of every European country was stronger than it was before the war.

That situation was a "God-send" for US companies. As European nations recovered, so did their demand for American made products. American investors were also active. Before the war they had concentrated on domestic projects, but after the war, looked overseas as well, including the oil rich Middle East. Arab states needed capital and technical know-how to open new fields. And American oil men were happy to oblige.

Underlying these activities was a conviction among US policy makers that the global economy was a key to America's security. Trade would make nations mutually dependent, diminishing the likelihood they would resort to conflict. Now America's economic vitality was also a key to containing Soviet expansionism. After World War II the Soviet Union had orchestrated communist takeovers in Poland, Hungary, Czechoslovakia, and other countries in Eastern Europe. President Harry S. Truman responded with a policy of containment. The West, led by the United States, would contest Soviet expansionism at every turn.

Military power was part of that strategy. In 1949 the United States took the lead in creating the North Atlantic Treaty Organization, or NATO a defense alliance that included 10 Western European countries, and Canada. NATO's first Secretary General said that the alliance was formed to keep the Russians out and the Americans in. Americans were indeed in, in Europe.

300,000 US troops were permanently stationed there. Whereas, the United States had fully demobilized after World War I, it did not do so after World War II, maintaining a large military establishment, and a permanently high level of defense spending. Even today, the United States spends far more on defense than any nation.

More than four times that of China, the next highest spender. Containment policy also aimed at keeping the Soviet Union out of the global economy. The Soviet economy would be marginalized, denied access to Western capital, technology, and markets. In the long run, that proved decisive. When the Soviet Union collapsed from within in 1991 it did so largely because its economy was in shambles. America's post-war strategy also included financial support for developing countries.

The US took the lead in forming and funding the International Monetary Fund, or IMF, which makes short term loans to countries experiencing economic problems, and the World Bank, which makes long term development loans to poor countries for capital investment projects, such as dams, highways, factories.

These financial instruments, along with direct US financial aid and investment were aimed at helping developing countries expand their economies, which would increase the demand for goods made in the United States, and elsewhere.

In these various actions, the United States acted as had no conquering power in world history. Rather than seizing the territory of its defeated enemies it helped them rebuild. Yet, there were some dark chapters too. In 1953 in Iran, and a year later in Guatemala, the United States helped sponsor coups that replaced democratically elected leaders with military dictators. In each case, the coup came at the demand of business firms, an oil consortium in Iran, and United Fruit in Guatemala, that had been exploiting the host country, and had been more tightly regulated when the elected government came into office.

Now, by the 1950s Americans were in the midst of a period of sustained growth and prosperity. US firms were still producing more than 40% of the world's total goods and services, and good paying jobs were plentiful. Nevertheless, America's post-war economic position was unsustainable. As the European and Japanese economy strengthened, they increasingly looked to sell their goods in foreign markets. By 1960 Germany accounted for a 6th of industrialized nations manufacturing output. Japan's productivity was lower, but by 1970 it was accounting for an eighth of the output.

In other words, America's trading partners had also become its trading rivals.

As you can see from this chart, the United States through the 1960s, was a net exporter, meaning it was selling more goods abroad than it was importing. By the early 1970s, the US balance of trade had leveled out. Each year since, the United States has had a negative balance of trade, consuming more goods from abroad than it was shipping overseas.

The 1970s were also a tipping point in other ways. As the Vietnam War dragged on the limits of US military power had become clear. The Korean War, two decades earlier, had ended in stalemate. And Vietnam would end with an American defeat. President Richard Nixon declared that the United States would no longer act as the free world's lone ranger, fighting localized wars to contain communist threats that posed no immediate danger to America's security.

Nixon also sought to reduce tensions with the Soviet Union. He initiated the Strategic Arms Limitation talks, or SALT which resulted in cutbacks in the US and Soviet nuclear arsenals. Then in 1972, Nixon visited the People's Republic of China, the first official contact with that country since the communists seized power in 1949. The Vietnam War also contributed to a major change in US economic policy. The war had produced budget deficits and sparked an inflationary spiral, prompting Nixon to take the United States off the gold standard in 1971.

Up to that point a country could demand gold for the dollars it had accumulated through trade with the United States. By eliminating the gold standard, the United States would not face that burden. The price of the dollar would now be determined by its value relative to other currencies.

Its value would float, going up or down, depending on the strength of the nation's economy and those of other nations. Given the dollar's position as the world's leading currency, the advantages of letting it float easily outweighed the advantages of pegging its value to gold. US policy makers didn't have to worry that other nations would refuse to accept paper dollars. They were in demand everywhere.

Moreover, the US now had greater flexibility during economic downturns to pump paper money into the economy without worrying that it would drain the nation's gold reserves. In addition, devaluation of the dollar was a way to improve the balance of trade. When the dollar depreciates it drops in value relative to other currencies, which means that goods made in the United States are less expensive abroad. By the 1980s, the American and world economies had changed fundamentally from what they were in the years immediately after World War II. There was vastly more market competition between countries and business practices had evolved. Business firms had become international players in their own right.

Changes in communication and transportation had made it easier for them to conduct operations without regard for national borders. A firm could be headquartered in New York with its factories in Thailand, giving it the best of both worlds. Access to management and finance in New York, and access to low wage workers in Thailand.

Why pay high wages to American workers when the same goods could be produced less expensively abroad and shipped back to US markets? An obstacle to the success of this production strategy was tariffs. Tariffs are taxes imposed on imported goods. High tariffs on goods produced abroad could wipe out the savings from making them there. America's multinational corporations began to pressure lawmakers to adopt free trade agreements, which would reduce or eliminate barriers to trade, including tariffs.

They found a rhetorical ally in Republican President, Ronald Reagan, who declared, "Our trade policy rests firmly on the foundation of free and open markets. I recognize the inescapable conclusion that all of history has taught. The freer the flow of world trade, the stronger the tides of human progress, and peace among nations."

Nevertheless, Reagan's rhetoric wasn't quite matched by his actions. For instance, he successfully persuaded Japan to voluntarily restrict its auto imports as a means of protecting domestic US automakers.

Economists were also preaching the benefits of free trade. Their research showed that free trade was a net economic gain for industrialized countries, largely because the job losses to lower wage countries were more than offset by the savings to consumers of lower cost consumer goods, such as TVs, clothes, and cars. A survey of US economists found that seven in every eight agreed that the United States should eliminate remaining tariffs and other barriers to trade.

A third force behind the push for free trade was the increased power of Republican lawmakers, who, because of their party's ties to business, are more supportive than Democrats of free trade.

In the 1960s and 1970s congressional Republicans were far Outnumbered by Democrats. But by the early 80s they had staged a strong comeback. They had taken control of the Senate and had narrowed the gap in the house. Developments elsewhere also added to the momentum behind free trade. European nations were on a path to economic integration, a passport free Europe, with few tariffs on trade. As a result, trade between European countries was increasing, with American products being squeezed out, because they were more expensive.

Upon taking office in 1989, President George H.W. Bush committed to negotiating a trade agreement that would serve as America's answer to Europe. It was NAFTA, the North American Free Trade Agreement, a trade compact involving the United States, Canada, and Mexico.

NAFTA would result in the immediate elimination of a wide range of the three nation's tariffs, and the gradualism of nation of nearly all the rest. Bush lacked the authority to implement NAFTA on his own. Congress has constitutional authority over tariffs and commerce with other nations. So, it would have to approve the agreement. That was not a sure thing. Free trade can look different to a member of Congress than it does to a president.

From a White House perspective, free trade is a winning formula, in that it is likely to boost national economic growth. To members of Congress, on the other hand, free trade is a question of its impact on their constituency. Although most members of Congress say they support free trade in principle they don't always do so when confronted with an actual trade agreement.

If the agreement will harm a major interest in their district or state they sometimes opt for protectionism, the use of tariffs, or other trade barriers to protect the domestic company from foreign competitors.

As it happened, President Bush was no longer in office when NAFTA came up for a vote in Congress. He had lost his bid for a second presidential term, the Democrat Bill Clinton. That complicated the issue. With their ties to business, Republican lawmakers tend to be strong advocates of free trade. Democratic lawmakers tend to be less supportive because of their ties to labor groups, which regard free trade as a threat to jobs. Organized labor had come out strongly against NAFTA, believing that American jobs would be lost to lower paid Mexican workers. Labor groups threatened to withhold election support from any democratic lawmaker who backed NAFTA. Environmental groups, another democratic constituency, were also opposed, citing Mexico's weak environmental protection laws.

Nevertheless, after studying the issue, Clinton came out in favor of NAFTA, concluding it would foster economic growth. Said Clinton, "NAFTA means jobs. American jobs. And good paying American jobs. If I didn't believe that I wouldn't support this agreement." Clinton's support was crucial. If Clinton, instead of rallying democratic members of Congress to support NAFTA, had vigorously opposed, it might have been defeated in Congress. And even if it had passed, Clinton could have vetoed it. When NAFTA was voted on in Congress in 1993, it had an overwhelming Republican support in both chambers.

Enough support from the democratic majority in each chamber to pass easily, even though the House vote was somewhat close, 55 percent in favor to 45% opposed. A similar scenario played out in the case of the three most recent major trade agreements. Pacts with Colombia, Panama, and Korea. They were initiated by the second President Bush, a Republican, like his father, and passed into law when a Democrat, Barack Obama, was President.

Obama argued that the agreements individually and collectively would increase American exports, benefiting US firms, and workers alike. All three agreements passed Congress in 2011. Each had the overwhelming support of Republican lawmakers, and enough support from congressional Democrats to pass comfortably. In each case, though, the vote was much closer in the house than in the Senate. Now, why do you think that was the case?

Do you think it was closer in the house mostly because the house has traditionally played a much smaller role than the Senate in foreign affairs, and thus house members are less likely than senators to take a national perspective on foreign policy issues? Or do you think it's because house members represent a district within the state, whereas senators represent the entire state?

It is the second one.

House members represent smaller constituencies there is a greater likelihood that a particular interest will be a large part of its economy.

If such an interest is adversely affected by a trade agreement the house member may oppose it. Here is a map that shows the district by district house votes on the Korean trade agreement. Notice the large number of no votes in Southern Virginia, and in North and South Carolina. Most house members from these areas, Republicans as well as Democrats, voted against the Korean trade agreement. These geographical areas contain much of what is left of America's textile industry. The Korean trade agreement was a threat to this industry because Korea is a leading textile manufacturer. And their products will have a price advantage over American competitors if the tariff was eliminated through the trade agreement. In fact, the cost and benefits can be concentrated, that is, focused on a particular interest. Or they can be the diffused, that is, spread across the society. The Korean trade agreement would impose costs on textile firms while the benefits would be diffused across the consuming public. Elected officials are wary of backing such policies. That get little credit for doing so while risking loss of support from those hurt by the policy. In 2017, in one of his first acts as President, Donald Trump killed a free trade agreement that had been negotiated by the Obama administration.

It would have created a trading partnership involving the United States and 10 other countries bordering on the Pacific Ocean. Trump claimed the agreement would result in huge job and manufacturing losses. Opponents criticized Trump as shortsighted, noting that the decline in the US manufacturing sector began decades ago, and is due largely to factors other than free trade. They claim that the main effect of killing their agreement would be higher prices for consumers.

Opponents also had another argument, one based on national security, for why they viewed Trump's action as a mistake. The free trade agreement would have linked the United States more closely with a number of Asian countries, helping to offset China's growing presence in that region. In the past decade, China has greatly expanded its economic reach, including sponsoring infrastructure, and commercial projects in Asian countries, for the purpose of drawing them into its sphere of influence. To a lesser extent, China has been pursuing the same strategy in Africa, South America, and the Middle East. The relationship between China and the United States is complex. For one thing, the American and Chinese economies are closely tied. China accounts for a sixth of all US trade. Roughly 80% of that trade consists of imports from China. Only 20% is accounted for by US exports to China.

That trade imbalance has existed for years, with the effect that China holds more than $1 trillion in US treasury bonds, the largest such holding in the world. China's growing wealth has enabled it to enlarge its Navy. It was structured to protect China's territorial waters but is being reconfigured to operate throughout the Pacific Ocean.

In recent years, China has aggressively pursued claims to islands held by Japan, Vietnam, and the Philippines. In 2014, for example, it deployed its Navy to protect the Chinese rig drilling for oil in waters off the coast of Vietnam. China has pointedly refused to recognize international laws governing the oceans and has laid claim to waters far beyond its coastline. China's claim is set forth in its so-called, nine-dash-line, which runs down the full length of Vietnam, nearly to Malaysia, and then back up past the Philippines. In response to China's actions. The United States has enlarged its Pacific fleet, and recently signed a mutual defense treaty with the Philippines. Nevertheless, it is unclear whether a serious provocation by China would be met with a forceful response from the United States. That option seems almost unthinkable, given the importance of China to the US economy. It seems unlikely that China would want to start a fight with the United States. Although its Navy is expanding, its vastly over matched by the US Navy.

China, for example, has one aircraft carrier, while the United States has 10, plus two in reserve. China's growing use of military and economic power is reminiscent of the path the United States followed after World War II, when it leveraged its military and economic power to shape the world in ways more to its liking. But there is a difference between today and then that many analysts believe will allow China's rise to power to be a relatively peaceful one.

The old system that the United States replaced after World War II was based on imperial rivalries that contributed to the Franco-Prussian War of the late 1800s, and then to world wars I and II. That system had been set up in a way that blocked the rise to power of any country that threatened the existing power structure. The international system that the United States helped construct after World War II is designed differently. It is meant to be inclusive, to allow nations to emerge, and be welcomed into the larger world community. In fact, China has already benefited substantially from that system.

When it opened itself to world markets it unleashed a massive economic growth that has brought it to the position it holds today. Rather than being blocked by the West, China has been asked to be a full partner in the international community.

It has been granted a seat on the UN Security Council and has been admitted to the WTO. Today's system is probably the thing that is most likely to keep China on a peaceful path. It can realize its ambitions by working within the system's rules and institutions. Let us summarize what is been said in this book.

We began with a look at developments after World War II, where the United States had overwhelming military and economic power and used it to create a global trading system, and to assist in the reconstruction of countries devastated by the war. They gradually emerged as trading rivals, as well as trading partners of the United States. By the 1970s America's dominant position in world trade had given way to a more evenly balanced system. It was also a time when the United States reached out to relax tensions with the Soviet Union and China. It took itself off the gold standard. By the 1980s, pressures for free trade, coming from business firms, economists, and political leaders, were building.

In 1993 Congress passed the country's first major free trade agreement, the North American Free Trade Agreement, NAFTA. The momentum toward free trade has slowed recently over concern about its impact on American firms and jobs.

Nevertheless, free trade remains a component of US foreign policy, stemming from the notion that strong trade relations, in addition to their economic benefits, draw nations closer together, diminishing the likelihood of conflict between them. I ended with a look at US China relations, noting their economic interdependence, but also noting their rivalry for power, particularly in the Asia-Pacific region.

I suggested that if that rivalry remains peaceful, much of the credit will go to the inclusive international economic and governing system that the United States helped create after the Second World War. It was here on an April morning more than two centuries ago that the American colonists first fought the British, starting their journey to becoming a separate and independent nation. Though it would take another eight years for the colonies to rid themselves of British rule, the war that started here marked the founding of a new form of government one based on the consent of the governed, rather than the dictates of a king.

"We the people" are the opening words of the US Constitution. The United States in 1775 was sparsely populated. It had a population of less than 3 million people. Communication was painfully slow.

It took days for a message to go from Boston to Philadelphia by horseback, and weeks for it to go by ship from Boston to Savannah. The United States today stretches from the Atlantic Ocean to the Pacific, from Canada to the Gulf of Mexico. It is home to 325 million people.

It has 25 metropolitan areas that have populations as large or larger than did the original United States. As for communication, it is instantaneous. How do you govern a country that big, that complex, that connected, that diverse? That is the question I have explored throughout this book, and that I will recap. I discussed the concept of power the ability of an actor to influence policy or control the behavior of others. Power is central to politics. Actors with enough power can oppose or cut taxes, start or stop wars, you name it. I am going to use power as a way to review what we have covered. I will talk about the power that is exercised through rules, institutions, ideas, knowledge, money, and citizens. Let us start with the power of rules. There is an old saying, known as the golden rule of politics those who make the rules get the gold. Now, that is literally and sadly true for some countries. Zimbabwe was once one of Africa's most prosperous countries.

Today, Zimbabwe's economy is a wreck.

Its wealth has been plundered by a corrupt regime, that after taking power in the 1980s, rewrote the rules that enrich itself. But the rules are important in every governing system. In the American case, the basic rules were devised by the writers of the Constitution.

They sought to limit power, dividing it between the legislative, executive, and judicial branches, in order to keep absolute power from falling into the hands of a tyrannical leader or majority. That rule, the separation of powers, sets the United States apart from most democracies. They have parliamentary systems where the majority party has full legislative control. But the American system requires the House, Senate, and president to agree before legislation can be enacted.

That rule can make it difficult for the majority to govern, unless, as in the 1960s, one party controls the presidency and has overwhelming superiority in the House and Senate. But when the parties are closely matched, legislative deadlock can result, as we have seen in recent years. On the other hand, America's system of divided and fragmented power is a boon to interest groups. I suggested earlier that the American system is as close to interest group heaven as it gets. Lobbying groups have countless points of access: House members, senators, the White House, the executive agencies, even the federal courts.

That is different from a parliamentary system, where group access is limited because power is concentrated in the hands of a few top leaders. The difference is the chief reason the United States has far more lobbying groups which wield far more power than do other democracies. The rules also explain why the United States has a two-party system. Most democracies employ proportional representation. Under that rule, parties win seats in proportion to the percentage of votes they receive in an election. It is a system that enables smaller parties to compete for a share of power. In contrast, the United States uses a single-member district system of election, which advantages big parties. A party has to finish first in a district in order to win the seat. A party that repeatedly comes in third or fourth gets nothing, which discourages smaller parties from competing. Now, rules differ in how precise they are. Some are rigidly defined. Others are more open ended. And that can affect how power gets distributed. A case in point is federalism, the division of sovereignty between the national government and the state governments. American federalism is an imprecise rule. As I explained in the federalism system, the US Constitution does not list the powers of the state governments. Instead, the 10th Amendment reserves to the states the powers not held by the federal government. So, the issue of state power is a question of the limits of federal power. That arrangement has contributed to the gradual expansion of federal power.

The Supreme Court's interpretation of Congress's commerce, and taxing, and spending powers has enabled the federal government, in response to changing national needs, to reach into areas traditionally controlled by the states. Through federal grants and aid to the states, for example, Washington now has a large say in health, education, and welfare policy. Under the rules of federalism, states can refuse to accept a federal grant.

But if they take it, they must abide by the conditions set down by Congress. The point I am making is this-- rules affect the distribution of power. So, to do institutional arrangements. Governing institutions are dynamic rather than static. They change as conditions change. And some institutions are structured in a way that makes them more adaptive than others. The presidency is an example. Although the writers of the Constitution expected the president to provide national leadership, its main job was to administer the laws passed by Congress. And that's how most early presidents saw their job. As President James Buchanan said, "My duty is to execute the laws and not my individual opinions." No modern president has looked at the job that way. As America went from a rural society to an urban and industrialized one, the federal government took on additional policy responsibilities.

Congress, because of its fragmented structure, was ill suited to overseeing the executive branch as it expanded to hundreds of agencies and hundreds of thousands of employees. Congress had no choice but to cede most of that oversight to the president. In 1939, for instance, Congress created the Executive Office of the Presidency to help the president oversee the bureaucracy.

The EOP today has nearly 2,000 staff members and 11 units, including the National Security Council, the Office of Management and Budget, and the Council of Economic Advisers. I will give you an example of how the EOP exercises its oversight function. But the staff resources available to the president through the EOP have also enabled the president to engage in a level of policy analysis and planning that is beyond the capacity of Congress. And it is become increasingly important as policy issues have grown in complexity. It is a reason, along with the president's unitary executive authority, that the president has become the source of most major policy initiatives, though on paper, that would seem to be the job of Congress. The presidency has also benefited from changes in technology and in America's international role. We live today in a world where security threats can materialize overnight from almost anywhere on the globe, and where the United States has the military power to respond quickly. These developments have shifted power to the presidency.

You may recall from an earlier discussion what Senator William Fullbright, a leading congressional critic of the Vietnam War, said of the presidential office. "It has been circumstances which have given the executive its great predominance. An entire era of crisis in which urgent decisions have been required again and again, decisions of a kind that Congress is ill equipped to make.

The president has the means at his disposal for prompt action-- the Congress does not." That development has weakened the Constitution system of checks and balances. The United States has gone to war scores of times since the end of World War II, usually by a sole order of the president, even though Congress has the constitutional power to declare war. Congress, as I noted, has no foolproof way to limit the president's war power.

Now, Congress remains a powerful institution. It has the lawmaking authority and the power of the purse, extraordinary powers in any age. Congress is supremely designed through its committee system to handle scores of issues simultaneously. Early in its history, Congress instituted the committee system, and gave committees the power to write legislation, a power that is denied committees in many of national legislatures. But relative to the president, the demands of modern government have worked to Congress's disadvantage.

Here is one more example of how institutional structure can affect an actor's power. The Supreme Court today is a far more powerful institution than the writers of the Constitution envisioned. Now, how did that come about? One reason is that the judiciary is a separate branch. The other two branches have a say over the Supreme Court. The president nominates, and the Senate confirms its justices. But once on the court, justices, in effect, serve for life.

That places them largely beyond the control of the other branches. Then too, the Constitution expresses the court's power in general terms. It grants the court the authority to hear all cases arising under the Constitution, federal law, and treaties. That is a broad mandate when one considers that much of the law is imprecise in its wording. The Constitution, for example, grants Congress the power to regulate commerce among the states. But what is meant by the term commerce? The Constitution doesn't say.

How does commerce among the states, which Congress is empowered to regulate, differ from commerce within a state, which it is not? The Constitution doesn't say. So, who decides the meaning of such words? It's the courts. Furthermore, the Supreme Court, early in its history, when it was housed in the Capitol building, assumed a power that is not explicitly granted it by the Constitution.

In Marbury v Madison, the court struck down an act of Congress, and in the process claimed for itself the power of judicial review, the authority to judge whether officials are acting within their constitutional power, and if not, to nullify their action. That is a powerful position to be in. The US system splits power between three branches and between the national and state levels, while also creating a dividing line between the power of government and the rights of individuals. Each boundary is a source of dispute, and the Supreme Court has the final say. As Justice Charles Evans Hughes noted, "We are under a Constitution, but the Constitution is what the judges say it is."

That is a significant power, and it was a basis for my claim in the judiciary, that the Supreme Court is an unusually powerful court. Institutional structures matter. That is clear. So, do ideas. Politics is typically portrayed as a game of strategy and ambition, not as a realm where ideas count. But as economist John Maynard Keynes said, "Ideas are more powerful than is commonly understood." Keynes authored one of those ideas, the theory that government, rather than cutting back on spending during an economic downturn, should spend freely in order to stimulate the economy's recovery. Keynesian theory, first applied during the 1930s Great Depression, prompted scholars and policymakers to re-evaluate the government's economic role.

That led economist Milton Friedman in the 1950s to devise monetary theory, the idea that the amount of money in circulation can be adjusted to slow down or speed up economic growth. Monetary theory has altered the distribution of power in Washington. It turned the Federal Reserve, the Fed, which was a low-profile institution before it assumed responsibility for monetary policy, into one of Washington's most visible and powerful institutions.

No set of ideas, however, has had a greater impact on American politics than those on which the nation was founded-- liberty, equality, individualism, self-government. Those ideas were voiced in the Declaration of Independence and became the basis of America's political culture. It is impossible to understand American politics without taking the nation's founding ideas into account. In this book, I pointed out the difference in how Americans and Europeans look at the issue of helping the needy. Americans are more inclined than Europeans to think that people should take care of themselves, a reflection of their belief in individualism. The difference between Americans and Europeans is reflected in a range of policies, including social welfare. Although the United States has a higher poverty rate than do most European countries, it spends less money on programs for the poor. The rules of welfare eligibility also differ. In most European countries, for example, all citizens are entitled to government-provided health insurance.

In the United States, individuals must prove that they are poor before receiving government help in obtaining insurance. Individualism's impact can be seen in other ways as well, including income policy. Compared with other Western democracies, the United States has lower tax rates, particularly on those of high income.

As Yale University's Robert Lane noted, Americans prefer market justice to political justice, meaning that they strongly prefer to have society's benefits distributed through the workplace rather than through government policy. Equality as an idea has also had a marked effect on our politics. America's promise of equality helped fuel the abolitionist movement, the suffrage movement, the black civil rights movement, the women's rights movement, and the gay rights movement. Now, these movements did not succeed solely because they were fueled by a powerful idea. Successful political movements require commitment, leadership, and resources. A movement also needs legitimacy, which is more easily achieved when its goal is aligned with a powerful and widely held idea. Ideas gain added power when encased in law. If liberty and equality had been expressed only in the words of the Declaration of Independence, they would still have had an impact on the nation's political development. But they gain power when they were encased in constitutional amendments.

That has enabled the Supreme Court to issue a series of rulings that have greatly expanded our right to speak freely, to obtain a fair trial, to be treated equally in law, to be protected not just from action by federal authorities, but from action by state and local officials as well. Yet another source of power is knowledge. In the past, I claimed that knowledge is power. You may recall the words of Ted Sorensen, a top advisor to President Kennedy. "The essence of decision is choice. And to choose, it is first necessary to know." No matter how simple a policy issue may seem, it usually has layers of complexity. Recognition that the United States has a trade deficit with China, for example, can prompt policy change.

But it doesn't begin to address basic issues, such as the form the new policy should take and the impact of a policy change on other issues, including national security. So, who exercises power through knowledge?

Well, as we've seen in this book, lots of actors do, including the president's policy advisers, the expert staff on congressional committees, the lawyers that litigate Justice Department cases, the economists at the Federal Reserve, the policy experts housed in universities and think tanks. The power of knowledge can be illustrated by looking at the budgetary process, the steps the federal government goes through in enacting the annual budget.

Each year, all federal agencies, and there are several hundred of them, must have their budgets renewed. The process starts with the OMB, the Office of Management and Budget. OMB has the task of issuing guidelines to each agency, including a budget ceiling that it cannot exceed. How does OMB develop these guidelines?

Well, the president is a source of guidance. OMB is part of the Executive Office of the President. But the details? Well they are largely worked out by OMB's professionals, its economists, policy analysts, management specialists, and budget experts. Now, after OMB has completed its work, the agencies dig in, deciding how to allocate their funding across their various programs and activities.

Key decisions are made at this point, and they are driven by bureaucrats' knowledge of their agencies. Whereas the president and members of Congress are policy generalists, bureaucrats are policy specialists. Many of them spend their entire career in the same agency, where they gain a thorough knowledge of its programs. Bureaucrats' knowledge gives them power during the budgetary process. As I indicated on the bureaucracy, bureaucrats have an agency point of view. They are committed to their agency and use their knowledge to shape its budget in ways that protect it.

Now, after the agency budgets are complete, they are combined into the executive budget that the president submits to Congress each January.

Congress has the final say on the budget, subject to a presidential veto. But members of Congress are not positioned to understand every detail in the budget. Although they acquire expertise through their committee work, the budget is massive. Members of Congress have only so much time and information. So, they turn for advice to the very people who worked out the agency's estimates, the bureaucrats? They are called before Congress to testify in budget hearings. Members of Congress also seek advice from the lobbying groups that benefit from agency programs. During our analysis of interest groups, I noted that lobbyists often have a better understanding of issues than do members of Congress. Lobbyists concentrate on a single issue, while the members must deal with many of them. Now, I am not suggesting that knowledge alone drives the budgetary process. The president and members of Congress have policy priorities, and they find ways to work them into the budget. But knowledge is a significant source of power in budget negotiations, just as it is in many other policy areas. Everything from trade agreements, to weapons systems, to antitrust action. If knowledge is power, a lack of it can be disempowering.

As political scientist Hugh Heclo notes, "Interests with a stake in a policy can be sidelined because they don't know enough about the issue to contribute meaningfully to the policy debate." Many policy issues are of this kind. For example, the American people have a stake in US policy in Africa, but know so little about the continent, that their opinions don't carry much weight. Knowledge is power.

So is money, and it works primarily to the advantage of business interests. In 1929, political scientist E Pendleton Herring wrote that "Of the many organized groups maintaining offices in Washington, there are no interests more fully, more comprehensively, and more efficiently represented than those of American industry." Although the lobbying scene in Washington's changed greatly since 1929, consumer and environmental groups, for example, are now a part of it. Business firms and trade associations still predominate. They account for roughly 2/3 of all registered lobbying groups.

When it comes to spending, their predominance is even more pronounced. Here is a list of the top 10 interests in terms of lobbying spending since 1998. Only one non-business lobby is on the list, the AARP, which represents retirees. The top entity, the Chamber of Commerce, has spent more than a billion dollars on lobbying since the late 90s. Election spending also has a business tilt.

One indicator is the number of PACs, Political Action Committees. You will recall that PACs collect voluntary contributions, and then donate them to candidates. Nearly 2/3 of all PACs are associated with corporations or trade associations. These PACs are also the heaviest spender, as you can see in this chart. Of the top 10 spenders in the most recent presidential election cycle, all but one was business related. The exception was the Credit Union Association, which represents the nation's credit unions, which by law are nonprofit institutions.

Super PACs tell pretty much the same story. You'll recall that Citizens United, the Supreme Court's 2010 ruling on campaign finance laws, opened the door to unlimited campaign spending by corporations, unions, and independent expenditure groups, provided they do not coordinate their spending with that of their preferred candidate. Super PACs are the outlet for multimillion-dollar contributors. During the last presidential election cycle, the top donor, Sheldon Adelson, who owned several gambling casinos, contributed nearly $100 million. So, what does all this money buy?

Well, it can give the lucky candidate who receives the money a boost-sometimes enough of a boost to win a close election. And for sure, money buys access, the chance to meet and talk with top policymakers. As one lobbyist said about the importance of his group's campaign contributions, "Talking to politicians is fine.

But with a little money, they hear you better." There is a final source of power to discuss. It is the power of citizens. Much of what I have said so far would suggest that ordinary Americans do not have much power.

Some observers believe that to be true. In his 1956 bestseller "The Power Elite," sociologist C Wright Mills argued that corporate elites effectively dictate the nation's economic policies. That conclusion is backed by a 2014 study conducted by political scientists Martin Gilens and Benjamin Page. They discussed nearly 1,800 policy actions, seeking through opinion polls and group activity to determine the pattern of influence. They conclude "Economic elites and organized groups representing business interests have substantial independent impacts on US government policy, while average citizens and mass-based interest groups have little or no independent influence."

That is a sobering finding. But it is not the full story. The power of ordinary citizens is less a question of the influence over a particular policy decision than it is a question of influence over the broad direction of government policy, a point I made. As I noted about the policy impact of political movements, they hastened the abolition of slavery, the granting of the vote to women, the dismantling of America's system of governing, the assimilation of women into the workplace.

Political movements are driven not by wealthy elites or business lobbies, but by ordinary people seeking a fair shake. Some of the largest changes in American society have come about when ordinary citizens have decided they have had enough of politics as usual and take to the streets.

As we discussed public opinion, noting how the direction, intensity, and salience of people's opinions can affect public officials. it is also true that citizens' opinions can keep issues off the table. An example is the Social Security program, which has such broad public support that it's protected from wholesale revision, a lesson that presidents Ronald Reagan and George W Bush learned the hard way. The power of people was also apparent as we discussed elections and political parties.

If there was any doubt about the importance of the vote, it would have been dispelled by the sweeping victory that voters handed Republicans in the 2010 congressional elections. In the two years before the 2010 election, Congress enacted several major bills, including the 2009 economic stimulus bill, the 2010 health care reform bill, and the 2010 Dodd-Frank financial reform bill.

After voters handed Republicans a huge victory in 2010, work on such bills stopped, replaced by work on bills aimed at cutting federal programs and spending.

The power of the vote was also evident in our discussion of party realignments, those periods when the parties reposition their coalitions and policies. What drives a party realignment? The answer is people.

A shift in popular support from the Republican to the Democratic Party during the 1930s Great Depression shaped the next three decades of American politics. The New Deal realignment brought with it a host of programs aimed at helping ordinary citizens, including Social Security, the minimum wage, Medicare, and Medicaid. My analysis on social issues also highlighted the public's influence.

Although economic interests have a large influence on economic policy, it is popular opinion, the opinion of the people, that drives issues like same-sex marriage, abortion, the legalization of marijuana, immigration, and race relations. I noted, for instance, the recent change in Americans' opinions on same-sex marriage, a change that accelerated the legalization of such marriages. A final example of the power of people is constituency influence on Congress. I argued that the inordinate amount of time and attention members of Congress give to the residents of their district or state, the extent to which their congressional staffs are engaged in constituent service, the tendency of members of Congress to deviate from their party when its position on a bill conflicts with that of their constituents.

Before summarizing this book, I would like to add that ordinary citizens have power in the American system, they do not have the power they deserve.

One reason is that whatever some officials may say, they are not interested in seeing large numbers of citizens go to the polls on election day. The United States has a long and ugly history of vote manipulation. Early on, property ownership was a voting requirement. After the Civil War, a whole new set of tricks, including whites-only primaries, were invented to deny black Americans the vote.

Women were not allowed to vote until the United States was well into its second century. Today, a citizen who wants to vote can face multiple hurdles-- long lines at polling places, because officials deliberately placed too few voting machines there. Registration offices that are hard to locate and frequently closed. And the requirement of a government issued ID as a condition of registration. The Supreme Court has been slow to disallow such practices. As vigilant as the court has been about free speech, it has failed to forcefully protect the right to vote. Yet, we also have not done our part. Turnout in US elections is far below that of nearly every other democracy, and at times, shameful.

In midterm elections, only about 40% of eligible voters show up at the polls.

If ordinary citizens are to exercise more power in America, we need to write a new chapter on voting as a right and as a duty. To recap this part, I have highlighted six sources of power. The first is rules. For example, how the US system of dividing power allocates power differently than does a parliamentary system, which works to the advantage of interest groups, but can weaken the majority's power.

The second is institutions. I noted that institutions are dynamic, rather than static, with the result that changes in conditions can alter an institution's power. An example is the presidency, which is institutionally better suited to the demands of modern policymaking than is Congress. We then discussed the power of ideas, noting that theoretical ideas, such as fiscal and monetary policy, and principled ideas, such as liberty and equality, have more power than is commonly assumed. I shifted to the power of knowledge, where through a look at the budgetary process, pointed out the influence of expert and specialized knowledge on policy. Fifth, discussed the power of money, indicating that business and wealthy interests wield inordinate power through their lobbying and election activities. Now, I would like to look at the power of citizens, suggesting that their influence is best seen by looking at broad developments, those resulting from political moments, party realignments, and major shifts in election outcomes and public opinion.

"Money is power" in the American system. Explain some of the ways that money is used to exert influence and who benefits as a result. the influence of money in politics works primarily through lobbying and elections. The major beneficiary is business interests. Business firms and trade associations account for roughly two-thirds of all groups registered to lobby in Washington, D.C.

When it comes to spending, their predominance is even clearer. Nearly all of the top spenders on lobbying are business firms and trade associations. They also have a large role in campaign spending. One indicator is the number of PACs-Political Action Committees. PACs collect voluntary contributions and then donate them to candidates. Nearly two-thirds of all PACs are associated with corporations or trade associations. Such PACs are also the heaviest spenders. Nearly all of the top PAC spenders are business related. Super PACs tell pretty much the same story.

Citizens United, the Supreme Court's 2010 ruling on campaign finance laws, opened the door to unlimited campaign spending by corporations, unions, and independent expenditure groups, provided they do not coordinate their spending with that of their preferred candidate. Super PACS are the outlet for multimillion-dollar contributors, nearly all of whom made their money in business and contribute to candidates who promise to promote business interests.

Citizens have a number of ways in which they exert power. Describe some of them. The power of ordinary citizens is less that of influence over a particular policy decision than of influence over the general direction of government policy. One example is political movements, such as the civil rights and women's rights movement. Such movements are driven, not by wealthy elites or business lobbies, but by ordinary people seeking a fair shake. When they succeed, they bring about substantial changes in society and policy. Public opinion also affects policy, particularly in those cases where it is intense and unmistakable, as in support for social security.

The power of people is also apparent when, as in the 2010 midterm elections, they handed Republicans a huge victory, thereby ending the Democrats' control of both the presidency and Congress, a development that changed the national policy agenda. Citizens' power can also be seen in party realignments, which involve large and permanent changes in the party coalitions and platforms, as in the case of the New Deal realignment of the 1930s. It is the movement of voter support between the parties that fuels a realignment and it is the continuing attachment of these voters to the party of their choice that sustains a realignment. A final example of the power of people is constituency influence in Congress. Members of Congress are inordinately attentive to constituency opinion, given the fact that they depend on their constituents for reelection.

Left Blank

Government Glossary

Affirmative Action: Programs aimed at giving women, minorities, and other disadvantaged groups equal opportunity in employment, education, and other areas of life.

Agency Capture: Situation where a government regulatory agency, rather than protecting the public, serves the interests of the industry it regulates.

Agency Point of View: The tendency of bureaucrats to adopt their agency's perspective and try to protect its programs and budget.

Appellate Jurisdiction: Authority of a court to review a case previously heard in a lower court.

Bad Tendency Test: Legal standard that says First Amendment does not protect speech that has a "tendency" to incite unlawful activity.

Block Grants: Federal grants-in-aid that give states and localities discretion in how the money will be spent within a general area, such as education.

Candidate-centered Campaigns: Campaigns where candidates are in charge of organizing the election effort and choosing the issues on which they will run.

Categorical Grants: Federal grants-in-aid to states and localities for a particular purpose or program, such as a school lunch program.

Caucus: A meeting in which voters discuss and openly vote for their preferred party nominee.

Civil Liberties: Fundamental individual rights, such as freedom of speech, that are protected from government infringement.

Civil Rights: Right of every person to equal protection under the laws and access to society's opportunities and facilities.

Clear-and-present Danger Test: Legal standard that says First Amendment does not protect speech that poses a clear and present danger.

Cloture: A Senate procedure to limit debate that requires a three-fifths majority.

Concurring Opinion: Opinion written by a justice who votes with the winning side but disagrees in whole or part with its legal argument.

Confederacy: Government system in which sovereignty (final authority) is vested entirely in subnational (state) governments.

Constituency: The people represented by an elected official.

Containment: A doctrine, developed after World War II, that the U.S. would contest efforts by the Soviet Union to expand its influence.

Cooperative Federalism: The situation where federal, state, and local governments work together to solve problems.

Demand-side Policy: Increase government spending in order to give consumers more money to spend, thereby increasing demand.

Derivative: A financial instrument whose price depends on the value of the assets it contains.

Direction (of an opinion): Whether people favor or oppose something.

Dissenting Opinion: Opinion written by a justice on the losing side that explains the reasons for disagreeing with the decision.

Distributive Policy: Policy that benefits one group while spreading costs across the full public.

Dual Federalism: Constitutional doctrine based on idea that a precise separation of national and state power was possible.

Earned Income Tax Credit (EITC): A tax credit for people who work in low-paying jobs.

Economic Class: People who share the same economic status.

Economic Efficiency: Relationship between economic output of what is produced and economic input what goes into producing those goods and services.

Economic Equity: Situation in which outcome of economic transaction is fair to each party; for instance, if the seller knows a product is defective, the buyer should be told of the defect.

Economic Groups: Groups organized primarily for economic reasons but that engage in political activity to further that interest.

Economic Sanctions: Punitive economic actions against a country taken by another country.

Electoral College: Each state has electors equal in number to their number of Senate and House members; the candidate who wins a majority of electoral votes is elected president.

Electoral Votes: Method for choosing the president, where each state has electoral votes equal in number to the number of its members (House and Senate) in Congress.

Entitlement Program: An individual benefit program, such as social security, that requires government to provide a designated benefit to qualifying individuals.

Evangelicals: Religious adherents who accept the Bible as authoritative and believe in spreading the Gospel.

Exclusionary Rule: Legal principle that evidence gathered by unconstitutional means normally cannot be used against the accused in a trial.

Executive Agreement: Treaty-like agreement made by president that doesn't require Senate ratification.

Executive Office of the President (EOP): The staff organization (includes personal assistants, specialists, and policy experts) that assists the president in carrying out major duties.

Executive Order: Presidential directive specifying how a law is to be carried out.

Fairness Doctrine: A government policy (rescinded in 1987) that required broadcasters to cover political issues in a neutral and balanced way.

Federal Grants-in-aid: Federal cash payments to states and localities for programs they administer.

Federal Reserve: The nation's country's central banking system, which is responsible for the nation's monetary policy by regulating the supply of money.

Federal System (Federalism): Governmental system in which sovereignty (final power) is divided between the national and subnational levels of government.

Filibuster: A tactic whereby a minority of senators prevent a vote on a bill by exercising their right to talk without limit.

Fiscal Federalism: Use of federal grants to states to extend the reach of the federal government into policy areas traditionally reserved for the states.

Flaw in Pluralist Argument: Some groups, particularly business firms, get the large share of the benefits from group activity.

Free-rider Problem: Situation where the benefits offered by a group to its members are available without charge to nonmembers, reducing their incentive to join the group.

Free Trade: Situation where tariffs and other trade barriers between nations are kept to a minimum.

Great Compromise: The compromise of small and large state delegates to the Constitutional Convention to create two chambers of Congress—one (the Senate) apportioned by state and the other (the House) apportioned by population.

Greenhouse Effect: Environmental warming that results when an increase in number of carbon particles in the atmosphere blocks heat from escaping into space.

Imminent Lawless Action Test: Legal standard that says First Amendment does not protect speech aimed at inciting lawless action if such action is both imminent and likely.

Implied Powers: Powers implicitly granted Congress by the powers granted it in the Constitution.

Information Commons: Situation where most citizens are regularly exposed to a more or less common version of the news.

Intensity (of an opinion): how strongly people feel about something

International Monetary Fund (IMF): Institution that makes short-term loans to countries experiencing economic problems.

Invisible Primary: Period during nominating campaign when, though no votes are cast, the candidates try to put in place the elements of a winning campaign.

Judicial Activism: The philosophy that courts should promote fundamental constitutional principles, even if such action conflicts with precedent or the policies of elected officials.

Judicial Restraint: The philosophy that courts should act with restraint, deferring generally to precedent and the policies enacted by the people's elected officials.

Judicial Review: Power of courts to decide whether a legislative or executive institution has acted within its constitutional authority and, if not, to nullify its actions.

Jurisdiction (of a committee): Policy area in which a particular committee is authorized to act.

Majority Opinion: Legal opinion put forth by a majority of justices as basis for their decision.

Mark Up: The authority of congressional committees to change the content of a bill.

Marshall Plan: U.S. initiative that provided billions of dollars to rebuild Europe after World War II.

Means Test: The requirement that applicants for public assistance must prove they are poor in order to receive it.

Medicaid: Government-provided health insurance for those with low incomes.

Medicare: Government-provided health insurance for qualified retirees.

Memory Tip: You aid the poor (Medicaid) and care for the elderly (Medicare)

Merit system: Hiring of government employees based on competitive examinations or special qualifications.

Moral Hazard: Situation where a party takes a risk knowing it can transfer that risk to another party.

NAFTA (North American Free Trade Agreement): Trade agreement involving the United States, Canada, and Mexico.

National Interest: The idea that countries should pursue policies that promote their security and well-being.

Nationalization: The historical shift in power in America's federal system toward the national government.

NATO (North Atlantic Treaty Organization): Military alliance of the United States, Canada, and most European countries.

Negative Externality (Spillover Effect): Situation that results when firms or consumers fail to pay the full cost of producing a good or service—for instance, when production results in air or water pollution.

Original Jurisdiction: Authority of a court to be the first to hear a case.

Oversight: Congress's constitutional responsibility to see that the executive branch faithfully administers the law.

PAC (Political Action Committee): Organization through which a group raises voluntary contributions and gives the money to election campaigns.

Party-centered Campaigns: Campaigns where political parties choose the nominees, organize the campaign effort, and determine the platform on which their candidates will run.

Party Polarization: The situation where political opinions and actions divide sharply along party lines.

Party Unity: Degree to which members of same party vote the same way on bills.

Pluralist Argument: Society consists of a large and diverse number of groups. As long as many of these groups benefit from group activity, that activity contributes to the public good.

Plurality Opinion: In the absence of a majority opinion, the legal opinion put forth by most of the justices on the winning side as basis for their decision.

Policy Implementation: The primary function of the bureaucracy. It refers to the process of carrying out the decisions of Congress, the president, and the courts.

Political Culture: The widely shared and deep-seated beliefs of a nation's people.

Political Socialization: Learning process through which people acquire their political beliefs, opinions, and values.

Political (Social) Movement: Sustained effort to achieve social and political change by people who feel government is unresponsive to their interests.

Poll Tax: A tax citizens had to pay before they could register to vote.

Pork-barrel: Legislation whose benefits are targeted at a particular legislator's constituency.

Power: The ability of an actor to influence policy or control behavior.

Poverty Line: As defined by government, the income level below which a family is defined as poor and thereby eligible for certain forms of public assistance.

Precedent: A judicial decision that serves as a guide for settling subsequent cases of a similar nature.

Preemptive War Doctrine: Doctrine holding that U.S. can attack a potentially threatening nation even before the threat materializes.

Primary: An election in which voters cast a secret ballot for their preferred party nominee.

Primary Election: An election in which voters directly choose the party nominees (rather than the party organizations).

Private (Individual) Goods: Benefits that a group can grant directly and exclusively to its members.

Progressive Income Tax: A tax on personal income where the tax rate increases as income increases.

Proportional Representation System: Electoral system in which legislative seats are allocated to each party in proportion to its share of the popular vote.

Protectionism: Use of high tariffs or other trade barriers to protect domestic firms and workers from foreign competition.

Public Assistance Programs: Social welfare programs funded through general tax revenues and available only to the financially needy.

Public (Collective) Goods: Benefits that are available to everyone, whether they belong to a group or not.

Quantitative Easing: An unconventional monetary policy in which a central bank creates money in order to buy securities from banks in order to increase their supply of money.

Reapportionment: The reallocation of House seats after each census to reflect changes in state populations since the previous census.

Redistributive Policy: Policy that imposes costs on one group to give a benefit to another group.

Regulatory Policy: Policy aimed at regulating business, carried out through regulatory agencies, such as the EPA and FTC.

Relative Deprivation: A sense of being disadvantaged relative to another group or groups.

Reserved Powers: Powers granted to the states under the Tenth Amendment.

Restraint of Trade: Business practices designed to eliminate or restrict competition in order to charge artificially high prices.

Salience (of an opinion): How important people think something is relative to other things.

Sample: A group selected from a larger population for purpose of estimating the population's characteristics.

Sampling Error: Error resulting from using a sample to estimate the population.

Selective Incorporation: Process by which selected rights in the Bill of Rights (such as the right to an attorney) are incorporated into the due process clause of the Fourteenth Amendment in order to protect them from state action.

Separated Institutions Sharing Power: Power is divided among separate legislative, executive, and judicial branches, each of which shares in the power of the others in order to serve as a check on their power.

Service Sector: Sector of the economy that provides services rather than products.

Single-member Plurality District System ("first past the post"): Electoral system in which only the candidate who gets the most votes in a district is elected.

Social Insurance Programs: Social welfare programs, such as social security, that require individuals to pay into the program in order to be eligible for its benefits.

Sovereignty: Supreme (final) governing authority within a particular geographical area.

Standing Committees: Permanent congressional committees with responsibility for a particular policy area, such as agriculture or foreign affairs.

Strategic Arms Limitation Talks (SALT): Negotiations between U.S. and Soviet Union to reduce their nuclear arsenals.

Supply-side Policy: Cut taxes on business and upper incomes in order to encourage investment in production, thereby increasing supply.

Tariff: Tax that a country levies on goods shipped into it from another country.

Three-fifths Compromise: Each slave would count as three-fifths of a person for purposes of taxation and representation.

Unit Rule: Awarding all of a state's electoral votes to the candidate who wins the state's popular vote.

Unitary System: Government system in which sovereignty (final authority) is vested solely in the national government.

Voter Registration: Requirement that citizens register beforehand in order to vote.

World Bank: Institution that makes long-term development loans to poor countries for capital investment projects such as dams, highways, and factories.

World Trade Organization (WTO): International organization through which its member nations negotiate rules of trade, such as copyright protection.

Writ of Certiorari: Decision by the Supreme Court to accept a case heard in a lower court.

References & Sources:

Not in Alphabetical order

Religion and Politics Since 1945, The Concise Princeton Encyclopedia of American History.

Thomas E. Patterson, "We the People", read the pages on religion and political socialization.

Michael Hout and Claude Fischer, "Explaining Why More Americans Have No Religious Preference: Political Backlash and Generational Succession, 1987-2102," Sociological Science 1 (2014): 423-444. Rather than focusing on the impact of religion on politics, this article examines how politics has elected Americans' religious practices.

Larry M. Bartels, "What's the Matter with What's the Matter with Kansas?" Quarterly Journal of Political Science 1(2006: 201–226. An analysis of how class and social issues relate to Americans' party loyalties.

Ordering Information:

Contact distributors for special discounts on purchases by academic institutions, nonprofits, and others.

Printed in the United States of America